A Young Person's Guide to Philosophy

An Introduction to the Ideas of Eastern, Western, and Contemporary Philosophers

By Avery Sharma

Table of Contents

Introduction

Everything has a beginning. From the first pebble on the ground to the first question or poem about the pebble. Just like the pebble had a beginning, so did the philosophers in this book. The dawn of philosophy started thousands of years ago when the sun rose in China in 551 B.C.E. at Confucius's birth. Confucius is considered the first philosopher in the history of philosophy and wisdom. However, many argue that Plato was the first since he focused on Western philosophy.

From the cliffs on the coast of Greece to the open ocean rife with sea monsters and nature spirits, philosophy has been a part of our lives before any of us or our ancestors were born. The Greeks who started asking questions led the example of trial and error, and the way they answered these questions helped the philosophers (or questioners) after them, from the Romans, Arabs, Western Europeans, and across the ocean to the East. The art of asking questions has been a part of us since we learned what a question was. As a philosophy book, this book teaches you about:

- the importance of the history of knowledge and thought from different regional perspectives

- wisdom as a force to be reckoned with if given the right tools

- justice as a way for your government to protect you

- freedom to do what you want to do as long as it doesn't harm others

- ethics to tell wrong from right and what to do about it

- religion as a way to understand our world while combining logic with faith

- reality and how this isn't a given, even in your dreams

- past lives and how you can become a better person by being kind

- how playful spirits can help your philosophical journey

- discussing current issues using a combination of past and present philosophies

Your history teacher might say, "Dates are important!" and they are, but what happens when the person and their legacy are remembered despite not knowing when they were born or the year they died? This is the nature of philosophy: People are important because they started asking questions. If the same questions are still asked today, do the exact dates really matter? In a way, they do because giving something a date means we understand the historical significance of the event or person.

In this book, you'll learn about dozens of philosophers, their ideas, questions, and philosophical legacies. I specifically left out dates in most of the chapters because people generally become fixated on a date when they see it instead of focusing on the information. This is like when you focus so much on the date your school holiday starts; everything the teacher says after that goes out the window. This happens to everyone, including the philosophers in this book. They were too focused on practicing their philosophies and often didn't bother writing the dates in their notes.

Even so, dates can be important because they help us understand the world around us at specific times. As you come across each philosopher's name, feel free to return to this page to get a better understanding of when that thinker lived compared to the philosophers before and after them. It could be a few years, a decade, a century, or even a millennium (that means 1000, not one million. Confusing, I know.).

When a year ends with B.C.E. (Before the Common Era), it means the date was a long time ago, before a formal calendar was adopted to record time. Time was still kept (otherwise, all of the dates would be the same), but when the Romans took authority in Europe, they changed the dates to reflect the birth of Jesus Christ. So what we call the Common Era starts in the year 1 and continues all the way to the year 2024 (so far). But the years before Jesus was born (the B.C.E. years) are counted backward. Imagine a number line that starts at the year 1. If the time period you are studying is 500 B.C.E., it means that it was 500 years before year 1, so you would count backward down the number line! The larger the number in B.C.E. dates, the farther away that year was from today.

Let's start way back, from the beginning of philosophy:

Philosopher:	Birth:	Death:
For Example:		
Confucius	551 B.C.E.	479 B.C.E.
Confucius's teacher, Lau-Tzu	571 B.C.E.	500 B.C.E.

Lau-Tzu was born in 571 B.C.E., and Confucius was born in 551 B.C.E. Lau-Tzu was older than Confucius because 571 is greater than 551. Lau-Tzu was 71 when he died (571-500), and Confucius was 72 (551-479).

Philosopher:	Birth:	Death:
Hesiod	750 B.C.E.	700 B.C.E.
Pythagoras	570 B.C.E.	490 B.C.E.
Shakyamuni (the Buddha)	563 B.C.E.	483 B.C.E.
Heraclitus	540 B.C.E.	480 B.C.E.
Socrates	470 B.C.E.	399 B.C.E.
Xenophon	430 B.C.E.	354 B.C.E.
Plato	428 B.C.E.	347 B.C.E.

Aristotle	384 B.C.E.	322 B.C.E.
Cicero	106 B.C.E.	43 B.C.E.
Seneca	4 B.C.E.	65
Marcus Aurelius	121	180
St. Augustine	354	430
Al-Kindi	801	873
Ibn-Sīnā	980	1037
St. Anselm	1033	1109
Ibn Rushd	1126	1198
St. Thomas Aquinas	1225	1274
Thomas Hobbes	1588	1679
René Descartes	1596	1650
John Locke	1632	1704
David Hume	1711	1776
Jean-Jacques Rousseau	1712	1778
Immanuel Kant	1724	1804
Georg Hegel	1770	1831

John Stuart Mill	1806	1873
Simone de Beauvoir	1908	1986
Freya Matthews	1979	Still asking questions!

With these dates, not all philosophers are spoken about with as much depth or detail as the next. Particularly for the early philosophers, the only information we have about them is what someone else wrote about them. If their scribe (a person, usually a child, whose job was to write about their lives and write letters) didn't think something was important, they would have left that information out. Later philosophers didn't usually have this problem because they could write about their lives themselves, but that also meant that they weren't always accurate about their lives.

People experience their lives based on what they have personally seen and heard. If their experience has taught them that writing about eggs means that very few people are going to read their work, they change their focus and start writing about puppies or kittens. Who doesn't want to read about that? I know I do! The information about each philosopher might not have puppies or kittens in the text, but I'm sure you'll find it just as interesting!

As you start on your philosophical journey, remember to ask questions and think outside the box. If there is an apple tree in your garden, but the tree doesn't make blossoms, don't ask why the tree doesn't make blossoms. Ask the roots of the tree if they have enough nourishment. When you nourish your brain, you take on the philosopher's approach and realize not everything is as simple as night and day.

To start your philosophical journey, you should choose a blank notebook as your first philosophy book. In this book, you can write down your thoughts on wisdom with the answers to the questions in this book. There are questions at the end of every chapter except Chapter 10, where you get to turn your questions into activities to practice philosophy!

Happy thinking!

A Note to Parents

Your child's philosophical journey has just begun, but this journey never ends. This is a good thing! Give your child as much room to grow as (safely) possible, and I hope you enjoy the "why" questions your child probably asks daily. Their questions will only get more involved as they grow into their philosophical brain.

There is an activity section in Chapter 10: Questions and Activities. Please encourage your children to answer the questions in the chapter (they can answer them in whatever order they like) and help them make philosophy a part of their daily lives by completing any of the activities (again, in whichever order they choose) based on the questions from each chapter.

Don't be shy regarding the questions for the activities. Each question adds versatility for the important themes and allows for many multi-use questions and answers. This might be important if you aren't part of an education system (teacher, caregiver, or principal) because questioning activities might not come naturally. If your children are old enough, they could also set their own activities based on the questions. This will allow you to quiz them afterward and pay attention to how they think compared to how you might have thought at their age. The activities have guidelines instead of direct instructions to help you understand that the activities don't have to be set in stone.

As a philosophy book for children, many of the concepts and phrases could seem complicated or over their heads. This is somewhat understandable: Philosophy was started by old men whose job was to protect their community. At the time, children were seen as the property of their parents with little to no autonomy. This makes philosophy for children a difficult subject because none of the philosophies or political doctrines of the past considered children as part of the community. They were only a part of the community when they contributed, which means as an adult.

For example, with religious philosophy, parents in ancient times didn't give their children a choice regarding their religion. This meant that the child grew up following a specific set of religious and moral rules without an opportunity to disagree. As a result, philosophy for children might seem very adult-oriented. It's up to us to help children understand what philosophy is from a young age so they can form educational opinions of their own. Only when we do this can our children participate in the philosophical discussions that influence their lives.

In philosophy, there is something called a "philosophy ache." This is when you (or your child) study philosophy and experience a headache or feel a bit tired. In philosophy, we change our ways of thinking and how we argue, and this puts extra pressure on how we think from a biological level. The connections (neuron to neuron) we once had based on what we previously believed are changed and, in some cases, broken. This happens so we can form new connections based on the new information we have and change our behavior accordingly.

Chapter 1:

The Birth Place of Western

Philosophy and Beyond

The First Greek Philosophers: Looking for the Answers

From the beginning of knowledge, there were people who asked the questions and people who found fragments of the answers. In history class, you might learn about the Parthenon, the Acropolis, or the Temple of Zeus. What made these places so important was the people who lived there when construction started. Ancient Greek philosophy was based on the lives of the philosophers, even though they weren't called philosophers at the time.

They were just like you and me: They asked questions and didn't stop until they were answered. The origin of Greek philosophy is passing knowledge down to help improve the understanding of the next generation. For the ancient Greeks, religion was also a part of their daily lives. It all started with Chaos, the first Greek deity and the parent of all the other deities. Deities are general gods or spirits who focus on people around them and nature rather than on worship and obedience, like the Christian God or Allah (the Islamic God). Deities were important in Greek society because they helped the Greeks answer the big questions about life, including:

- Why do we die?

- Why is justice important?

- What impact do we have on the nature around us?

- What impact do natural events like earthquakes and floods have on our lives?

- Why do earthquakes and floods happen?

The Greek origins of philosophy also relied on the natural world itself without the deities directly interfering in people's lives. For example, the deities wouldn't build roads for the people. Instead, they gave their people visions in their dreams to teach them how to build roads. The deities watched over the early people of Greece. They only intervened when necessary, passing their wisdom on to those who needed it. For example, if your parents lived in Ancient Greece and they had to understand how to build roads in the mountains to visit family, they would call for the deity Gaia, and she could answer by coming to them in a dream. In the dream, she would show them how to build the roads, and when they woke up, they would have gained that knowledge.

Philosophy can be seen in two ways: pre-Socratic philosophy concerning the philosophers listed below and post-Socratic philosophy concerning the philosophers listed in the remainder of the chapter and book. All four pre-Socratic thinkers wrote a lot about Greek culture and philosophy, and most people today know and understand philosophical words because of these questions. Our understanding of the impact of the deities on pre-Socratic philosophy came from the Papyrus Derveni, a document created by the pre-Socratic philosophers to help understand the world, and four important thinkers of the time, which include:

- Hesiod: He was a poet before he was a philosopher. Poetry was used to understand people's worlds. In his first work/poem, he used poetry to ask questions about the deities present in Greek philosophy and history and to answer questions like why people needed to follow the deities to live a good life. His other poem recounted his brother's life of crime and asked the question, why do we need justice?

- Heraclitus: Was the first pre-Socratic philosopher to focus on humanity outside the influence of the deities and spirits. He often asked whether or not people understand philosophy in the way it's meant to be understood—as information for the elite to give to the masses (people). By asking questions to those in charge, Heraclitus believed that all people have the same needs— the need for an identity. It's up to the leaders to ask their community what they believe their identity should be.

- Pythagoras: Didn't write anything down. No philosophies, ideas, mathematical theories, or questions. He instead focused on the Pythagorean Question. This answered the question of what would happen if a person and philosopher was stuck in the middle of knowledge and ignorance. Pythagoras asked philosophers to think about living without proof that things exist (like in math) and living without questions (like in exploring ideas). By answering his question, we can understand if a life without proof can be as happy as living without asking questions.

- Xenophon: Xenophon was misunderstood in an era where questions weren't encouraged. He asked questions about the Peloponnesian war, the brutality of man, and the reasons behind treachery. You can say Xenophon was the first pre-Socratic political philosopher. His questions about law, virtue, and loyalty paved the way for the later political philosophers to ask their questions about liberty and the state.

Many Fields, Many Philosophers

The fields listed below are a mixture of pre-Socratic (the deities) and post-Socratic philosophy (the philosophical fields). However, the most important pre-Socratic philosophy thinking comes from the Milesians. They were the first people to ask questions about the universe, including the questions asked by Hesiod, Heraclitus, Pythagoras, and Xenophon as above. For ancient people, where they lived and what they saw every day shaped their understanding of their world.

Athens was a maritime city (a city on the coast), and water was a part of everything the Ancient Greeks did. They used it for cooking and cleaning like in modern times, but they also used the sea water as medicine and a way to power their farming equipment. Water was their explanation for everything in their natural world (what they saw and heard every day), and their answer to the most important questions of the universe was the *arkhé*. The *arkhé* means the beginning or the source of everything the Greeks experienced. In Greek mythology, the *arkhé* is the special force that created the gods and the world. People have always wanted to understand where everything came from, and the *arkhé* shows us how ancient Greeks thought about the beginning of life and the universe. For the Milesians, science and philosophy were separated by the question: Is this water or not? This was the question of the *arkhé*.

Water was seen as the soul of the Milesians. Everything that contained water had a soul, so the *arkhé* could answer the important questions. Objects that contained water were people, plants, animals, and, of course, water. In pre-Socratic philosophy, where the deities and Greek people came from (who created them, where were they created, and why) relied on how much water was available for people to use: Water in their homes, how close they were to the ocean, and how much rain they had to help the plants and trees grow. Anything that didn't focus on water (like astrology) wasn't important, so they didn't speak about it. In this way, the Milesians were more focused on biology, chemistry, geology, and meteorology because they all contained water in some form.

In post-Socratic philosophy, the other fields were focused on because they placed less importance on water. All the important questions about life were asked by the Greek thinkers, and these questions are still being asked today. All these fields of study were seen as part of philosophy for the ancient Greeks because they focused on how you can apply what your teacher taught you. These studies included questions about:

- Biology: How life begins.

  o Associated deity: Apollo.

- Chemistry: How people reacted to ancient medicine.

  o Associated deity: Hermes.

- Ethics: The question of good vs. bad.

    o Associated deity: Dike.

- Geology: How mountains and islands are formed.

    o Associated deity: Gaia.

- Metaphysics: How we understand time and space.

    o Associated deity: None (metaphysics is a new field of philosophy compared to the others).

- Meteorology (what we now call astronomy): How the stars and moon align.

    o Associated deity: Zeus.

- Physics: How gravity works.

    o Associated deity: Physis.

- Psychology: How we understand the mind.

    o Associated deity: Hypnos

- Theology: How religions and deities impact our lives.

    o Associated deity: Also Zeus.

Creation Isn't Necessary

There isn't a specific historical moment or memory that created the ancient philosophies; it is just a collection of new information that was put together and spread to those who would listen. This information might not seem new to us because we know what philosophy is or at least know when to ask the right questions. New information about the ancient Greek philosophers is unearthed through archaeology and new translations.

The most important philosophical find of this time is the Papyrus Derveni. It helps us understand what type of lives Plato and Orpheus led and why their teachings are so important, even today. It was written long after Plato (50 years) and Orpheus (150 years) died, so it might not be 100% accurate. The lessons in this document are still important, though, because they help us understand why these thinkers are called philosophers today.

The Papyrus Derveni helps us understand the nature of the world as the original thinkers understood it. All the people, places, rocks, plants, teachings, and lessons in nature were seen as one thing. Before Plato, thinkers saw their world as a whole instead of separating people from places, rocks, plants, and teachings. Everything was seen as a single unit, like a tank at the aquarium—the fish need the water plants for oxygen, and the plants grow strong because of the plant nutrients in fish poo. (Gross, I know!)

The Greek Masters: Socrates, Plato, and Aristotle.

Finding the Arkhé in Socrates

Just like the *arkhé* started with the Melisians and the questions asked by the four founders of Western thought—Hesiod, Heraclitus, Pythagoras, and Xenophon—the concept of good, bad, and virtuous (good from a moral standpoint) had to start somewhere. For Western philosophy, it started with Socrates and his debates with his friends and colleagues. Socrates believed that to be good was to examine your life while learning without focusing on the answers to the questions themselves.

Socrates questioned the nature of philosophy itself, and philosophy became a way of life for him instead of something that could be learned in a classroom. Socrates lived in a time when democracy (a political idea where the elections are fair and everyone has equal representation) was only just starting in Greece. His teachings gave his students a way to understand and accept what was going on around them, even though it was new to them. He taught them how to think for themselves and make decisions based on fact and reason instead of ideas and superstition.

It was almost as if Socrates' teachings were specially made for democracy. The new democratic parties of Greece called themselves Sophists, and they encouraged people to support them by holding debates and discussions in private houses. They charged money for speaking to crowds and for people to watch their debates. Socrates agreed with a lot of what the Sophists did because he knew they had the power to change politics if necessary, but he argued that thought should be free.

Once the Sophists became more popular, Socrates distanced himself from the crowds and focused on one-on-one tutoring for people who agreed with him. He wasn't forgotten, though, and the people of Greece claimed he was the wisest man they knew. Just like a wise grandparent who tells you stories about their younger days and doesn't understand how important they are to you, Socrates denied he was the wisest man in Greece.

The Oracle of Delphi (a wise person who is the speaker of the deities) called Socrates the wisest man, but he still denied it because he claimed he didn't know everything. Socrates lived out the rest of his days teaching others about right from wrong before the leaders accused him of corrupting the youth.

Plato is one of the most well-known philosophers today, and he was a student of Socrates. Plato was also the primary writer for Socrates because Socrates didn't write anything down, so this makes it difficult for us to know what was Socrates' work and what was the work of Plato.

Imagine doing a group project for school and handing it in without telling your teacher who did what—your teacher wouldn't know who completed which part, so they would give you all the same mark. It's a little like that. Plato focused more on Heraclitus and Pythagoras, while Socrates saw all four men as a part of philosophy itself. The main similarity between Plato and Socrates is the use of dialogues (with individual people) and debate, which is what Socrates was famous for.

Plato: The Well-Traveled Philosopher

Plato was more aware of people and everyday life than Socrates, who mainly kept to himself and focused on politics and relationships rather than questions about the nature of things in general. Plato came from a wealthy and connected family, so his ideas spread more easily than those of his teacher. He was also well-traveled, which influenced his writing and teaching methods. This made it difficult for leaders to trust him. They didn't know if he was going to spread the same ideas as his teacher.

His travels allowed Plato to develop a philosophy that required more teaching than a single person could give, so he started an academy to spread his ideas and learn from other philosophers around the world. This academy was in Athens, and he spent the rest of his days there after he was exiled from Rome (where he visited to spread knowledge). Questions remain regarding his burial place because he wasn't found at the academy. Even in death, he kept people questioning.

Aristotle: The Student Exceeds the Master

Aristotle was the final ancient Greek thinker (now called philosopher), and he was a student of Plato. Aristotle is often called the father of modern scientific philosophy and scientific methods because of his diverse subjects and keen eye for arguments. Aristotle was heavily influenced by the pre-Socratic fields of philosophy and added a few of his own. By the time Aristotle entered the philosophical world, these fields were more developed. At the same time, they were seen as separate fields from philosophy except for ethics and metaphysics.

There was a new focus on the pre-Socratic fields but from a scientific perspective: Old problems were being solved using facts and reason, not opinion and the belief that water is the source of everything. Aristotle added to the pre-Socratic fields by focusing on the same ideas but with different meanings and without involving the deities. The fields he added or changed included:

- Biology: The study of plants and nature itself.

- History: The study of the past.

- Rhetoric: Using information to persuade others.

- Philosophy of mind: Reflecting on thoughts with reasons why things happen.

- Philosophy of science: Reflecting on thoughts with calculations and trial-and-error.

- Poetry: Understanding life with words and rhyme.

- Zoology: The study of animals.

Aristotle's father was a doctor for an important king of Macedonia, which helped his ideas gain popularity outside Greece compared to those of his predecessors.

From Greece to Rome: Cicero, Seneca, and Marcus Aurelius

Developing Cicero

Much like Socrates saw the rise of democracy in his time in Greece, Cicero saw the development and failings of the Roman Republic in his time in Rome. The Roman Republic followed a fair system that was like democracy, except that the leaders of the Roman Republic were elected by the votes of important families in the area. In Greece, the democracy Socrates saw was less fair because the leaders elected themselves but allowed the people to elect minor political figures who couldn't challenge their rule. Cicero was born into a wealthy family, which meant he had two choices for a job—soldier or lawyer. He disliked the military, so he studied law.

As part of his legal studies, he also studied philosophy because it had become a well-known field by this point. He took important legal cases so he could be recognized by the important people in Rome, and he focused on philosophical speeches when he argued his cases. He used philosophy to help him with his cases, using the knowledge passed down from the pre-Socratic philosophers and Aristotle. He often exaggerated his point and he annoyed the Romans with his arrogant nature.

By focusing on political philosophy and law, Cicero taught his followers and contemporaries that a state should be run according to what a good government can offer its people. His speeches in Rome emphasized his main philosophy: Those in power needed to prove they were worthy of making decisions on behalf of their citizens. As part of his speeches (which were similar to Socratic dialogues), Cicero argued that instead of using philosophy to explain the form of government, politics, and the law, we should examine the importance of philosophy as an applied method of thinking to understand the decisions made by the state and government.

Cicero believed his form of law and philosophy was the only form that should be taught in schools and universities. The Romans exiled him because they wanted to make him an example of what happens when you disagree with what they believed (which isn't very democratic). He wasn't allowed to live within 500 miles of Italy. Five hundred miles is a long distance today. When he was exiled in 58 B.C.E., 500 miles away was like the other side of the world, which made it very difficult for him to stay in touch with people who agreed with his philosophies.

Before he was exiled, he was famous because he wasn't afraid to take on difficult cases and was willing to stand against Rome when necessary. When he returned, he became infamous for daring to return at all. When he left, his followers and friends assumed he would die because of the distance of his exile. People generally didn't live to see the end of their days when they disagreed with the Roman Republic. Even though his following dwindled when he got back, those who supported him did so without fear, and they were the ones to start spreading his legacy of law and philosophy.

Seneca and Ancient Stoicism

Most of the modern philosophies you will read about in this book can be dated back to a Spanish philosopher called Seneca. He started the Stoicism philosophy, which states that you are responsible for focusing on your personality and way of life without worrying about what others think of you. Seneca taught in Rome. He wasn't well-liked by the leaders and even some of his students (do you see a pattern yet?) because he was violent, and he gave very different opinions on the same topics, which confused his students.

He differentiated between philosophy and politics like Aristotle, and his early writings were often seen as auto-biographical because he spoke about his early life and how he understood the natural world, compared to other philosophers who didn't put themselves in their writings. His separation of philosophy and politics helped him become an advisor to Nero, the Roman emperor. Nero was also violent like Seneca, and he didn't care about Stoicism or his empire; he only cared about his art.

Seneca tried to help Nero adopt Stoicism because his Stoicism focused on your will and how you see yourself compared to your friends, which he called "impressions." Agreeing or disagreeing with something you have been told shapes your will and helps you make better decisions in the future. By making better decisions, the impressions other people have of you will improve, and you will gain more friends because of your good personality.

Marcus Aurelius: The Philosopher-Emperor

Marcus Aurelius was a philosopher-emperor and the only one of his kind. He argued virtues are good, so you should focus on them, and vices are bad, so you should avoid them. To be virtuous, you must behave according to positive morals like kindness, charity, and honesty instead of becoming cruel, stealing, and lying, which are all vices. Marcus Aurelius came into power at the perfect time because a plague was spreading in Egypt, Germany, and Italy. Marcus's philosophy was also a type of Stoicism, and at the time, it was just what the people needed because it helped preserve peace by focusing on virtues.

Marcus Aurelius drew inspiration from Plato, Heraclitus, Democritus, and Homer, who were all important thinkers of the time, and they focused on the importance of the result instead of the small things that take time.

Everyday things like eating breakfast or playing with your friends wouldn't be as important to these thinkers compared to when you asked yourself important questions like "What is time?" "Is there fate?" "Why do we die?" or "What happens when we die?" "What are the cosmos made of?" and "What guides our sense of justice?" Marcus Aurelius also focused on the questions about good vs. bad from a religious point of view since Christianity was slowly replacing the Roman deities at the time.

Keep Thinking! Suggested Questions

You can start your questioning by getting a special book and only using it for your questions. Remember, there are no wrong answers to philosophical questions!

- Before you started reading this book, how much did you know about philosophy?

- What do you know about ancient Greece and Rome?

- What does the word religion mean to you?

- What is democracy?

- What does modern mean? Is it a time like a year, or does modern mean something new?

- What is science?

- What is violence?

Chapter 2:

Middle Ages: When Philosophy Meets the Church

Two Opposing Worldviews: The Aristotelians and the Islamic Scholars

Aristotelian philosophy was the next hot thing in the Western world, but on the other side of the world, many years after the teachings of Aristotle, the Islamic philosophers made strides of their own. At the time, Baghdad was at the center of education and philosophy, alongside Cordosa and Damascus.

In the Middle East, these cities were the talk of the town because they rivaled the Western scholars in mysticism, education, and equality. Those who traveled between Baghdad and Greece (including Aristotle himself) claimed the schools in Baghdad were a form of Plato's academies, and from there, the circles of philosophy exchanged ideas. It was like all the important thinkers studied in Baghdad before starting their own adventure in asking the big questions.

Aristotelian philosophy was studied by Islamic thinkers for centuries after his death, and they used the Aristotelian principles to critique and correct any flaws they saw in the later Aristotelian schools and as a guideline for their own religious philosophy. From an Islamic perspective, the fields of philosophy discussed by the pre-Socratic thinkers and Aristotle himself could be explained by religion and the will of Allah. Aristotle specifically left the deities out of his fields, and the Islamic thinkers believed this was his main flaw.

For Aristotle, his fields of philosophy didn't need divine intervention outside of what was taught as cosmology at the time. This is like your English teacher explaining an old book and how to solve the problems the characters are having in the story by talking about the weather—the clouds and storms might be interesting, but they don't change anything about what happens next in the story. In Islam, the clouds and storms from the story were created by Allah, so they were just as important as the characters themselves. The Islamic scholars struggled to support the Aristotelian views completely because of this. Even though the questions Aristotle and those in the Middle East had were the same, they had different causes and answers.

Not Everyone Agreed With Aristotle

People in Persia started to feel strongly against Aristotle's ideas because they wanted to protect the Islamic community from thinking about things that didn't include a god or important purpose. This way of thinking quickly spread to other parts of the Middle East. News of this feeling reached Greece, and philosophers in both areas felt attacked (not physically), and for the first time in the history of philosophy, two major scholastic groups were at an impasse in what was right, wrong, justifiable, and accepted. Jewish and Muslim scholars felt particularly attacked when important questions were answered in favor of reason instead of divine right, which ignited the burning questions in the Middle Eastern philosophical world.

The Aristotelian way of arguing and debating led to a conclusion without consulting the religious leaders for guidance, which wasn't a good enough argument for Islamic scholars. According to them, Allah already knew the answers to the burning questions, and it was up to the scholars to reason with one another and find the answer from within. At the time, Islamic thinkers didn't think of themselves as philosophers according to Western standards because their philosophies were already a part of their religion and culture. A separate field of philosophy wasn't needed.

The result of this was a two-way discussion of Western and Islamic philosophies where both sides accepted equally important questions, and these important questions might even complement one another. This didn't mean the questions said "You have a nice hat" to one another; it meant they could be answered while building on what was agreed on before. One important debate answered by the Islamic scholars in a similar way to the Aristotelians was that the history of the world and universe can't be understood by everyone because no one living at the time saw the world being born.

For the Aristotelians, the history of the world and universe was the field of cosmology without the influence of the deities. This is known as physics today because ancient cosmology and meteorology relied on deities controlling the earth and stars, but cosmology and physics rely on what we can test and prove to be true with our own eyes and instruments, something the ancient Greeks weren't able to do. This was also known as cosmology for Islamic scholars because Allah was present in the sky so he could watch over his people, which means this also falls under cosmology but for a different reason. This similarity fueled the discussions and critiques from both sides and a healthy competition of mystery and intrigue followed for decades to come. Unlike in Ancient Greece, the definition of cosmology included Allah and His influence on the world.

The Mixing of Ideas

In Greece, Islamic philosophies were introduced to the concept of marriage and the importance of women and girls in the home. Greek couples would simply live together and have children but focus on the men and boys when it came to education and manners because they were the only ones allowed to study. In the Middle East, girls and boys studied the same things, and women had an equal say in what happened in their homes. It wasn't like this in Greece during the Aristotelian era.

Many Western philosophers visited Baghdad to gain and spread knowledge, and the universities and some political and religious leaders in Baghdad took this information and used it to support Islam and the quest for knowledge in general. This new form of teaching was called the "new wisdom" (Rahman & Schimmel, n.d.), and it was a combination of Aristotelian ideas and Islamic principles. This type of philosophy was practiced in the Middle East until recently, and it challenged Aristotle's ideas on matter (the physical form of something) and form (the mental idea of something).

Instead, the Islamic thinkers argued that Aristotle's matter is the "light" of philosophy and that his forms are the "dark" aspects of philosophy. This type of mysticism is common in Islam, and it is related to how close people are to Allah. If you follow Allah's way of life, you will be closer to the light because Allah gave you "matter," but if you don't follow Allah's way of life, you move closer to darkness. Your form (mind) needs a strong idea to hold onto, but your idea will fall apart if you don't focus on it constantly, so it is un-formed in your mind. The "new wisdom" (Rahman & Schimmel, n.d.) gained a lot of popularity, and Islamic scholars spread it throughout Asia and India.

Proving God Exists: St. Thomas Aquinas and St. Anselm

St. Thomas Aquinas

St. Aquinas started his religious journey at a French monastery and studied as much as he could to prove the Christian God existed. Thomas was told to go home because the emperor (Emperor Frederick II) wanted to take over the capital of Rome. He wanted to control the Holy Roman Empire because it had a lot of rich areas. The Pope was worried because he thought he would lose power if all his helpers (the clergymen) left him. Back then, Christianity wasn't the main religion, and the Pope couldn't stop what Frederick was doing. After this, Thomas (he wasn't a saint yet) left and joined another Christian faculty called the Dominicans.

The Dominicans focused more on democracy and less on charity, which was the opposite of what the Pope believed. Faith through thinking hard and hard work helped Thomas find his place in the church and with God. He spent his days teaching fellow Dominicans about the Bible and preaching to whoever would listen to him. His parents had different hopes for him, and they didn't approve of him spending so much time in the church. He was only 14, so they believed he should help at home instead. Maybe the parents in ancient times weren't so different from the parents of today. The people in his church saw that he belonged with them and the church, so they persuaded his parents to allow him to study at university. His parents agreed when they realized it was the most famous university in the world at the time: the University of Paris.

At the University of Paris, he gained a following, which was the beginning of his philosophical life and the birth of evangelicalism. The Islamic and Western philosophies joined forces again at the University of Paris, where Thomas studied naturalism (from the Islamic scholars) and rationalism (from the Aristotelians). When he left university, he started writing and speaking his version of religious philosophy called Thomism. Like his Aristotelian predecessors, he was accused of corrupting the youth. Unlike those who came before him, he argued he had a way to prove God existed and spent the rest of his life arguing and trying to prove his theory. Aquinas had five proofs of God:

1. Motion: He argued that nothing can move on its own, and the moving force is God (even for people walking down the street).

2. An efficient cause: Thomas argued that everything exists for a reason, and the reason is that God created the "thing" and that the "thing" exists to do God's will.

3. Necessity and possibility: In nature, things are possible, or they are not, or things can possibly exist, or they can't. He argued that when God thinks something is necessary, he makes it possible for it to exist.

4. The size of something: If something is small but can become large (like a dry sponge compared to one filled with water), God is the reason that it can change its size.

5. Design: People and animals all behave according to what they will experience when they get old. Since God knows what will happen to you when you get old, He designs your life around

what will be the best option for you, and you act according to that will.

Think about it like this: If you see an apple and want to tell someone about it, what will you do to convince other people that it exists? You know the apple is there, but if your friends can't see it, you will need to prove it's there using language they understand.

St. Anselm

St. Anselm added to Aristotelian metaphysics and cosmology (through religion and divine guidance) and helped the church gain popularity when support was low. He was also a poet and many of his later writings were philosophical poems and hymns for the church. His early philosophies weren't always recognized by the church because of different opinions. He argued that religion and philosophy should be the same, but the church wanted to separate the two. His proofs of God helped him stay out of trouble with the emperors. They were still threatened by his presence, so he spent the rest of his days in the monastery, teaching those who would listen to his ideas and poems.

In France, St. Anselm also tried to prove God existed using other means, but he didn't start out that way like St. Aquinas did, and like St. Aquinas, he was only made a saint after he died. Anselm traveled a lot when he was young, and people called him a nuisance because he enjoyed starting fights. When his travels and mischief-making came to an end, he felt the calling of the church and found himself in the Benedictine monastery in Paris. He studied hard and was noted as an important scholar and teacher, which was very different from his early days! Like St. Aquinas, he was naturally gifted in theology, and he became well-known and recognized soon after he started his studies.

The monastery where he studied became the most important monastery in France at the time because it was the center of theology and philosophy, all controlled by Anselm. Philosophy and theology are what Anselm prided himself on. He was also very good at administration, which included organizing the correct paperwork, setting up meetings for important people, and arranging correspondence.

In Anselm's time, email and instant messaging weren't possible, and letters had to be sent in the post. It took a long time for mail to reach its destination because there were very few main roads, and the roads were full of people trying to steal letters to use as blackmail. Anselm's skills with correspondence allowed him and his colleagues to communicate with each other safely and in a reasonable amount of time. Imagine sending your parents a message, and they only get the message in a month! That would be very stressful for them, so they would want someone like Anselm to make sure their letter got to you in time before anything in the letter changes.

In his teaching position, his career and reputation thrived, and he was asked to become the Archbishop of Canterbury. This position was directly under the Pope, so people thought he was very important. He hesitated at first because of the politics in England at the time with the new king. This king, King Rufus, was just like Anselm was when he was younger (violent and seeking adventure), and Anselm didn't trust him.

He took the post in the end, but he realized he was right to be wary of this post: The King believed he should be involved in the religious duties of the country as well (at the time, this was England), and he fought with St. Anselm often regarding his decisions for the church. The king sent Anselm to Rome on official religious duties. While there, Anselm was exiled, and he returned to France, where he lived in the Benedictine monastery and continued to teach people about God and the church.

Anselm had his own proofs of God, and he wrote about these in his later years when he spoke to the youth. For Anselm, there were also five proofs of God, and many of them built on the previous one:

- Faith: Faith, according to Anselm, is the love of God, and he said that if you know God, you will love God, which proves he exists.

- The divine: Anselm believed that nature is divine because it was created by God, and the fact that nature exists is proof of God. A part of this divine reasoning relies on God being omnipotent (having unlimited power) and that God can't feel pain. In nature, God is powerful enough not to need other forces to control it, and we exist in nature to be uncorrupted by other forces.

- The last three proofs are linked—freedom, sin, and redemption: Freedom is the freedom of choice not to sin. God can sin because God is free, but he chooses not to, and that is proof that God exists. Redemption is something people can choose as proof that God exists because if God didn't exist, why would people want to redeem themselves and prove their goodness?

St. Anselm lived the rest of his days in France, having a quiet life with the church, teaching his proofs to those who would listen. If your teacher had to retire before they wanted to, it's not like they wanted to stop teaching. They will teach whoever will listen in that case, and that's exactly what Anselm did.

The Middle Ages and the Church: St. Augustine

St. Augustine was born Aurelius and was made a saint many years after he died. Aurelius was the most important theologian at the time because he was a direct connection between Rome and Platonic thinking. Platonic thought was gaining popularity because people wanted to go back to simpler times regarding politics and questions, and despite Aurelius having the least amount of exposure to Plato's works, he made the connections between Rome and Greece and founded his religious thought on that.

The Roman Catholic way of life was built on Aurelius's theories because he focused on freedom from Rome and fate from Plato. He came from a well-known family who focused on his education and connections. At school, he focused on rhetoric, and he was a good speaker, easily getting his views across to everyone, not only his teachers. When he finished studying, he returned home to raise his son and taught his son what he could. He was then forced into the clergy by people who knew about his impressive speaking skills, and as they had predicted, he excelled at this.

Aurelius focused on the orthodox beliefs of Christianity (following the early and original teachings of the Bible without modern interpretations) and the intellectual thought of the time regarding philosophy and the big questions. In his writings and speeches, he was able to write for everyone and teach them about Christianity and philosophy in their language, which helped his popularity and acceptance. Up until now, the only people who could read were priests, bishops, and kings and queens.

Aurelius disagreed with this because he thought everyone should be able to read religious books, and he started writing books in plain language for his congregation to learn from. These books used his form of Christianity (the combination of orthodox and intellectual), and his reputation as a religious philosopher allowed him to write and preach however he wanted. This is very important because a teacher or parent can learn all the facts of the world, but if they only speak in English in a classroom that only speaks French, the children won't understand them, which isn't the children's fault. If Aurelius were your teacher, he would speak in French to make sure the class understood the lessons and the meanings of the words he used instead of assuming the class would pick up on the lessons.

The words he used and how he used them were very particular, and his form of Christianity became a secular (didn't have to follow the general church rules) form, which solidified his place in the church. He was able to speak to people and help them when necessary without getting the church involved, which helped them because they could focus on their own mission (of charity and conversions). Aurelius had used his position as Bishop, the third most important person in the Christian church under the Pope and Archbishop, to spread his ideas and write for the church. His life wasn't without his own scandals, though. He often fought with people from his own secular religion when they disagreed with him. Not much else is written about him, and he likely died while still practicing his religion.

Keep Thinking! Suggested Questions

Remember, there are no wrong answers to philosophical questions!

- What is a worldview?

- What does the word divine mean to you?

- What is a scholar?

- Which area has more people, the Middle East or Greece?

- What is dark and light for you?

- What does proof mean to you?

- What does nature involve? Is it everything that is outside your home or only living things (like trees and bugs and stuff)?

Chapter 3:

Akl-Kindi and Islamic Philosophy

What Is Islamic Philosophy?

Islamic philosophy isn't understood in the same way as Western philosophy (the Greek, Roman, and religious philosophers you read about earlier). People saw Islamic philosophy as a way of life instead of something to be studied in a school or church. Islamic philosophy is tied to faith in Allah and the scriptures while existing in harmony with other people. In a way, Islamic philosophy is similar to the pre-Socratic era, in which everything from the natural world was included in the teachings and practice of the faith.

Faith and reason go hand-in-hand in Islamic philosophy because they build each other up: Faith is the belief in the scriptures, and reason is having the intellect to understand what the scriptures mean. As part of the Islamic faith, the combination of philosophy and science was discussed to understand the intellectual questions of the time. Unlike the pre-Socratics, however, these questions were asked to ensure the understanding of religious messages and guide the people of the Middle East towards Allah and the messages that were given to the people.

Islamic philosophy was and is a tradition of culture before a religious movement. Religion and theology are prized as part of this culture. Still, Allah was felt by the Islamic people in their everyday lives. As a result, there is less focus on active practice and praise throughout the day, which leaves Muslim people free from the time constraints of praying or worshipping. There is trust in Allah, the philosophies spread by the religious leaders, and the teachings of the prophet himself.

Think about it like this: If someone you trust (like a parent or close family member) asked you to do something, would you refuse because you have things to do, or would you do the favor because you know your trusted person wouldn't do anything to hurt you? Faith in Allah and the religious leaders is a little like that. They do the best for their people, so they give good religious advice and advice on how to live pain-free lives.

The Varied Lessons of Islam

Knowledge and faith are tied together in Islam because religious leaders study the information and knowledge passed down through the scriptures and translations, and they build and shape Islam from these passages. These passages help religious leaders combine faith and religion based on traditions passed down through generations while living in the modern world.

Islamic faith becomes Islamic religion and vice versa when those who practice faith (the love of Allah in this case) make their daily faith rituals a part of their society and everyday life. Religious leaders of Islam encourage their followers to pray and study the Quran as often as possible to welcome Allah into their lives. When people (including the people from ancient Middle-Eastern times) make these rituals of praying and studying a part of their lives, the Islamic faith becomes a religion.

If your family is religious, think about what you do to show your faith (it can be any religion, not just Christianity or Islam) in your home and daily life. Do you go to church or another religious building? What do you think the religious leader does when they get home? Do they practice the things they spoke about in the sermon? By making something a part of your daily life instead of thinking about it on a single day (like Sunday for Christian church), it becomes a religious practice instead of an act of faith when things get rough.

If your family isn't religious, think about something you do together that helps all of you feel better or lets you bond over special memories. This can be a weekly or monthly trip to the park, a Sunday roast at your grandparents' house once a month, or the trip to the beach you go on every year in the summer. These activities might not be religious, but they need faith from your parents to believe that they are possible. They need to know if they can drive to the places, have money to spend on the activity or trip, and take time off work to make it happen. These activities become a part of your family's "religion" because they are practices done at specific times and for specific reasons.

In Islam, the philosophies are so intertwined with their religion that it's difficult to separate Islamic philosophy from the Islamic religion. The lessons and teachings of the Islamic thinkers will help you understand why Islamic philosophy is so varied and bound to knowledge and reason compared to the early Western philosophies.

Important Islamic Thinkers: Al-Kindi, Ibn-Sīnā, and Ibn Rushd

The Life and Teachings of Al-Kindi

Al-Kindi, known as Alkindus in the West, was a part of a tribe called Kinda before he started his religious journey. Tribes in the Middle East didn't always have to follow the laws of the government, and many of them had their own leaders who traded with the cities for food and resources; many of these resources were books. Al-Kindi's tribe was close to the caliphate (the form of government at the time that combined religion and politics), so they had direct access to important religious and legal documents circulated throughout the city, and he was able to read these documents from a young age.

As it was the educational capital of the Arab world at the time, al-Kindi's parents sent him to Baghdad for schooling, where he started his life's work—translating legal and philosophical papers from Greek to Arabic. The friendships he developed in Baghdad formed the relationships he would need for his translation journey, and his main goal was to translate important philosophical and scientific papers to re-distribute to the important families of Baghdad and the rest of the Middle East.

These important families were encouraged to teach their subjects what these documents said in a way they would understand and by including Allah in their lessons about family and worship. In these teachings, the families were encouraged by al-Kindi to compare Western values with the values of Islam and explain why the lessons in the Middle East were better than those of the West.

Becoming a Philosopher

From a philosophical and family perspective, al-Kindi's teachings were focused around his mentor—a vital part of Islamic religion—al-Muʿtasim biʾllāh, and their focus on the meaning of words, animals, and psychology. Al-Kindi also studied and discussed cosmology and meteorology in terms of weather patterns and what he learned from Ptolemy, an Egyptian leader who was thought of as the mathematician of North Africa. With a lot of interests, Al-Kindi also studied mathematics, music, and medicine production. In general, al-Kindi's later philosophies focused on Aristotle, who he read about while translating his works. Al-Kindi's group of translators focused on charity as part of their philosophy, even though Aristotle didn't support charity.

Al-Kindi's first paper was the "First Philosophy," where he spoke about the knowledge of Allah as the first truth, which is different from Aristotle's first philosophy of science. Al-Kindi believed that Aristotle was worthy of Islamic praise because Aristotle understood that objects are one with the universe with his understanding of physics and astronomy. In Islam, objects are one with the universe because they were made by Allah, who is the universe.

Al-Kindi is thought of as the first Islamic philosopher because he was the first Islamic philosopher to ask metaphysical questions. The Islamic "philosophers" before him were called "thinkers" instead because they didn't ask questions outside what they were told to think about. Al-Kindi argued that Allah and the world are one, which was how people understood Allah and their world. Allah is a simple god because all he wanted from his people was for them to serve and learn about Islam and for Muslim people to be bound to him (another way of saying Allah can control them) so they could discuss what Allah can offer them in return for their faith.

34

The way al-Kindi thought about philosophy and its impact on Islam and vice versa is a bit like a math teacher who asks why $2 + 2 = 4$. If your teacher researches what the number 2 means and what it represents, they could answer their question by explaining that a grape can be split in half, so you get 2 sides. If you split 2 grapes in half, you will have 4 sides, so 2 (each half of the first grape) + 2 (each half of the second grape) = 4 because there are four sides. Your teacher doesn't have to ask why the first grape was a red grape and the second grape was green; the simple answer is that two halves of each grape equals four. If Allah were the grapes, He would still be Allah at the end of it because the simple math problem is how He wanted to be portrayed.

Ibn-Sīnā, the Mystic

In ancient Islam, philosophy and medicine weren't separated, which can be seen in the life and work of Ibn-Sīnā, also known as Avicenna in the Western world. Ibn-Sīnā combined Greek and Islamic philosophies to practice medicine and philosophy in the Middle East, and he re-introduced pre-Socratic philosophies to the West with his correspondence and among his Islamic allies. This was the opposite of al-Kindi. In a similar way to al-Kindi, Ibn-Sīnā created the opportunity for religious and philosophical questions based on his writings and ideas.

Before traveling to Baghdad, Ibn-Sīnā focused on theology, mysticism, religion (Islam and the ancient deity-worship of the pre-Socratics), and science. He became well-respected in his hometown of Bukhara, modern-day Uzbekistan, because of the questions he asked and the lengths he went to to answer them, which was constant debate (Socrates-style) and re-reading his works and the writings of other Islamic thinkers to challenge his opinion and what he already knew.

As education was highly praised in the Middle East, Ibn-Sīnā's father sent him to study in Baghdad when it became the center of culture and language. Around the same time he was sent to study, the powerful Samanid family rose to power and employed Ibn-Sīnā as a doctor and medical philosopher.

He was able to heal the Samanid ruler (although the history books don't specify what from), and as a thank you, he was allowed into the large library that the Samanid family owned. He wasn't given any teachers because the teachers were busy teaching the young Samanid children, so he prided himself on being completely self-taught. While studying in the library, Ibn-Sīnā broadened his horizons and studied astronomy, geometry, logic, mathematics, metaphysics, music, and physics. He expanded on al-Kindi's metaphysics even though he disagreed with his religious philosophies and was the first Islamic philosopher to study ethics and economics. Ethics and economics were partly the reason his writings and philosophies were so well received.

Think about your school and favorite subject: How do you think you would do if you didn't have a teacher for that subject? If all the teachers in your school were busy teaching everyone else, you might have to ask others to help you and make up your own tests. By doing so, you will learn things your teachers might have missed because they have to teach something specific for the year. By asking questions and testing your own knowledge, you can start learning about the bigger questions while learning about the smaller stuff.

Ibn-Sīnā focused on sharing his ideas so many people could learn from him. Because of this, Islamic ideas helped to inspire the Renaissance in places like Greece, Rome, and Paris. Translations of his works were made public, and the influential families had a second source of Islamic philosophy and thinking after al-Kindi. The way his papers were written made it easy for regular people to read them once educational opportunities became more available, and his teachings spread as far as India (1,822 miles from Baghdad).

The writings and lessons from Ibn-Sīnā followed the lives of everyday people instead of the religious figures who read the writings so the people could relate to the teachings more than ever. The discoveries Ibn-Sīnā made in medicine and theology changed the way medicine was thought of in the Middle East, and his views were widely accepted because his writings and correspondence gave the feeling of an understanding between the people and their religion. The role of the religious leaders as a guide to Allah instead of as a guide away from culture was welcomed as a counter to the Western form of culture and family. Ibn-Sīnā started his philosophy career as a political philosopher while teaching religious Islamic philosophies because of the impact of Allah on the lives of the people in the Middle East.

When Ibn-Sīnā was 21, his father died, and he had to return home to Bukhara to look after his family. The Samanid family had a presence there, and he was able to get a job in the government's economics and financial field. When the Samanid family lost power in Baghdad, Ibn-Sīnā had to choose between fleeing his home town or serving the new rulers in an economic position. He chose to stay in the city, and his works from Bukhara illustrate his understanding and wisdom in an equally important way of life: Islamic philosophy for the people and not the powerful.

Ibn Rushd, the Judge

Ibn Rushd, known as Averroes in the West, was the third vital Islamic philosopher and thinker after al-Kindi and Ibn-Sīnā. Like Ibn-Sīnā, he also focused on two fields of Islamic thinking other than theology and faith.

He was a judge and became well-respected in his field because of his fairness in cases and his ability to argue his points without trying to discredit the opposing thinker. This was common in the West, and although he agreed with the majority of Aristotelian views, he chose science, logic, and rhetoric to argue his points. Ibn Rushd thought about the issues relating to the Aristotelian problems, including the world existing without cause. This made spreading new philosophies in Greece difficult because people didn't know who to believe: Aristotelian beliefs or their town leaders.

Do you know what a judge does? If you do, why do you think they are called a "judge?" Do you think all judges should be fair? They should be, and with the knowledge Ibn Rushd gathered over his years as a judge, he was considered the fairest of them all (like Snow White without the evil stepmother!)

In Greece, Ibn Rushd was known as "the Commentator" (Ahmed & Pasnau, 2021) because the Greeks didn't realize Greece and Rome weren't the only places to develop philosophical thought. This didn't stop him, and his education gave him a considerable understanding of astronomy, ethics, medicine, logic, physics, politics, and psychology. The Greeks called Ibn Rushd "the commentator" because he wrote a lot about important topics and talked to them about how to make their society better. Given his extensive knowledge regarding the important questions and his writings, he easily created treatises (a formal document signed by countries or people where they agree on certain terms for how they are ruled and treated) as a judge, which paved the way (alongside those who came before him) for the founding beliefs of Islam and religious philosophy. Three treatises were used by religious leaders to share Islam with their people, and these are still studied today in Islamic philosophy:

1. Fasl al-Maqal: This focuses on the impact and value of all the philosophical components of religious Islamic philosophy and the lessons he agreed with in Aristotelianism. This treatise helped the general population understand Islam as a way of life instead of an activity.

2. Tahāfut al-Tahāfut: Involves the influence of Ibn Rushd's teacher and Islamic thinker, Ghazāli. The principles in this treatise focus on how Islam and Allah can philosophically answer Aristotelian questions (without the personal opinions of the religious leaders).

3. Al-Kashf 'an manāij al-Dilla fi 'aqā 'id al-milla (yes, it is a mouthful!): This treatise is partially responsible for the Shia sect of Islam. This treatise and believers in Shia argue that Allah is the only one responsible for appointing religious leaders in Islam based on their principles and philosophies, including the Prophet. This treatise and those before them naturally affected Islam because of the different views and opinions of those who follow Sunni law (like Ibn-Sīnā, who argued that the Prophet was Allah themselves).

Unlike the al-Kindi and Ibn-Sīnā, Ibn Rushd didn't have a mentor, so people believed his good nature and kind heart when they read or heard about it because they knew what he did and how he felt came from within and from Allah. Ibn Rushd also didn't have a biographer, so his life after his writings and treatises were lost to time.

Keep Thinking! Suggested Questions

Remember, there are no wrong answers to philosophical questions!

- What do you understand by the word "reason?"

- What is a leader?

- Do they have to be religious?

- What does something have to do to exist?

- What is a necessity?

- What is the Greek language called?

- What is a translator?

- What is charity?

- Did charity start with the church?

- What makes someone worthy?

- What is a library?

- What is a commentator?

- What is a guide?

Chapter 4:

Philosophy and Politics: Are

Human Beings Naturally Good?

What Is Human Nature?

From a philosophical and political perspective, there are mixed opinions on human nature. Some people argue that humans are biological beings only, relying on what we do with our bodies. Others believe plants and trees are a part of human nature because they give essential nutrients and support to our lives.

Relationships are important for everyone. The relationship you have with nature is one of the most important ones because it's a physical relationship with natural things like plants and animals (including your food), and it's also a psychological relationship where you only see what nature can give you in return if you do something nice, like not stepping on a bug. We can also see what human nature is from ethics and how we should behave around others. As people, we know what cruelty is (the opposite of kindness), and this makes us human. Another definition of human nature includes our friends. If we help our friends because they are kind (opposite of cruel), we will be a "human" because we helped someone else without asking for anything in return.

A Cruel Behavior

"Nature" in human nature has different answers depending on who is asking the question. The ancient Greek question of "What is nature?"

includes the Greek deities who played a big part in the pre-Socratic religions. The answer to this question will include anything created by the deities—people, plants, and animals. In this case, the "nature" in human nature means us and how we interact with the people and animals in our towns.

Nature can refer to human behavior, like good nature or bad nature. Nature characterizes how you behave without thinking about what your parents taught you because they can't change how you act toward someone. Your natural behavior toward someone is what you feel on the inside.

What do you think about humans in general? If they are kind or cruel, why do you think that is? Philosophers have thought about the meaning of what makes people kind or cruel (like a bully) since they understood what kindness and cruelty meant. For some philosophers, your personality is tied to your belief system or how well your parents taught you to avoid fights. If you haven't been taught how to care for someone, it's very difficult to be kind. If you have been taught that caring isn't necessary, a cruel nature might become important to you because you will only think of yourself.

Understanding human nature involves realizing what it means to be human as part of nature itself, like the trees and insects, and the nature of people around you who are kind or cruel. The philosophers in this book understand human nature differently because of how they were taught. Political philosophers see human nature as a link to the state of nature, which is a term that describes how people behave with their family and around their government. Others believe human nature should only include people in their natural environments, like their families (without worrying about the government).

What is More Important—Nature or the State It's In?

The state of nature is the state before modernization and the development of modern governments. It refers to the state people are in before learning how to behave in modern society, such as practicing kindness and using the bathroom. The state is also an invisible border called the state line, where rules and laws change between areas. The political philosophers who believed in the state of nature believed that the people before modern society were dirty, unclean, and uncooperative. To them, the state of nature is the actions of the people in the state from a geographical perspective.

Think about what kind of state you are in right now. Do you have a bathroom in your home? Are your clothes clean (or were they clean when you put them on)? Do you know screaming at the top of your lungs in public is rude? If you lived in a state of nature, all of these questions would either take you away from the state of nature or help you understand why nature and the state are the same.

Political philosophers argue that people in a state of nature need to move away from people who are bad influences and focus more on the gardens or forests of their land to avoid temptation. In a state of nature, people can't protect their environment and farms, which will lead to food shortages, and the gardens and forests will be overrun by people trying to persuade their friends to stop asking questions.

Living independently in the state of nature is important because being part of a group can lead to dangerous situations if your safety is at risk. For example, if your community doesn't allow a neighbor to eat or have a place to rest, the neighbor will become aggressive. Political philosophers who believe in the state of nature argue that people are naturally violent and aggressive because they are afraid their food and safety will be taken away. Because of this, the state of nature prioritizes survival over others' needs.

Is There a Violent Nature?

In the state of nature, people have rights tied to natural elements such as air, food, sunshine, and water. By making sure people have access to these rights, aggression and fear will disappear. Your survival is tied to how many natural elements are missing in your life. Air, food, sunshine, and water will help you meet your basic needs, so you won't need to fight anyone for them. By focusing on your basic needs, the police won't be needed because everyone will have the essentials. No one will need to be aggressive with anyone else to meet their needs. Justice exists in the state of nature, as individuals should behave themselves to avoid aggression and maintain their rights. Rights might look easy when we talk about things like air, food, sunshine, and water, but they are very important for other rights, too, because justice can help squash violence and keep people living together happy.

Hobbes, Locke, and Rousseau: Three Ways to Look at the State of Nature

Thomas Hobbes

A social contract theory is something all political philosophers have in common. It's a way of thinking that sets out political ideas and principles that emphasize how free the people are and what they are expected to do based on rational thinking. That might sound complicated, but it's not: The "social" part is what the people are expected to do to and with the other people around them, like not to steal from them and not to gossip about them. The "contract" part includes the ideas and principles set out by the state (as in government), and the "theory" part is how rational the people are based on what they know about themselves and other people in their community.

Hobbes believed a social contract theory that works for everyone involved should include the government (contract) as the only group of people making decisions on behalf of everyone else, also called absolute authority. He stated the responsibility of enforcing the state of nature should be up to the people and their moral code (social), and he also stated that people must accompany others when being taught about politics and morality (theory) to ensure the state of nature is being upheld.

Hobbes has three arguments about the state of nature because he thought that living freely didn't mean everyone would be safe. He believed that to keep people from being mean to each other, we need to make sure everyone is protected:

- In the first argument, Hobbes said that anything is better than war, so people in the state of nature should do everything they can to stay out of conflict.

- His second argument explained that in the state of nature, people are responsible for their own political outcomes and actions, and they have the right to defend themselves against people who get in the way of their responsibilities.

- The third argument is that the state of nature is in a state of war because people in the state of nature have different opinions of what the state of nature is. If people can't agree on this, they must leave the state of nature; otherwise, a war will start.

Do you think war and nature are the same thing? If you think about it, without nature, war couldn't exist because there wouldn't be a place for it to happen. If everyone could disagree with the government that sets the rules, the government would probably disagree with those who break the rules. That's where justice comes in.

John Locke

John Locke is considered a religious philosopher because he believed in God. Unlike the other religious philosophers discussed in this book, he didn't write anything about the proofs of God. Instead, he used God as the creator of people and the creator of the monarch (the ruler of a country who was put there by the royal family) as the religious head of a state to help people find their way. He argued that people are free by nature (personality-wise) because God gave them the freedom to follow the monarch. Locke argued that for true freedom, people need to have rights. The right to believe in what monarch they want to run their state (as in country) and the freedom to choose to be free instead of choosing a prison if they break the law.

As a political philosopher, Locke also had a social contract theory, but his contract was between the government and the people. He argued people use the social contract theory to give some autonomy (making decisions for themselves and by themselves) to the government for protection from the state of nature. Locke believed that people agree to have a government to help keep them safe. He also argued that this government should follow what people want, not just what the people in government want to do for personal reasons like make more money to buy more expensive things. He says that if there isn't a judge in charge to help guide things, everyone is left to take care of themselves, but they won't be fighting because the government will make sure their needs are met.

According to Locke, when people live together and can agree on a leader, their peaceful way of life will benefit everyone, so they don't have to change how they do things. If some people can't agree on a leader, they should leave the group to keep things nice and calm. Property played a big role in Locke's state of nature. There were some simple rules about how to take care of your things when people lived in the state of nature. Locke said you should use your things as much as you can before giving them away or throwing them out. You can only have something if you worked hard for it, so gifts or handouts don't count.

If you want to give something away or donate it, you need to have permission from the person who used to own it and from the person you are donating to. By asking for permission, you can make sure the person you are donating to understands that you worked hard for this and you want to share the work. When any of these rules were broken, Locke said you would be removed from the state of nature until consent was given by the government to return.

In the United States, each state (California, New Jersey, Virginia, etc.) can make up their own laws that the people have to follow according to what the government says is right or wrong. If Locke was alive today, he would say that each state is a political state in his state of nature because each territory has different rules. Areas like the European Union are different because each member (country) of the European Union has to follow rules that the governments set for the whole area (from Portugal to Sweden and the countries in between). A law they make in Portugal has to be made in Sweden because they are part of the same political territory—they are both part of the EU. If Locke was alive today, he wouldn't call the European Union a state.

In Locke's state of nature, religion plays a part because the government shouldn't enforce the state of nature. This will take away people's consent to how they want to be ruled. To avoid this, Locke said the government should be religious because they will have the authority to remove people's consent. As speakers of God on Earth, the religious government won't remove consent for the wrong reasons, like a non-religious government might to get back into the state of nature.

If the monarch is God's voice on Earth with the other religious leaders, wouldn't they need permission to use God's property (the crown for the head of the monarchy and the churches built by the monarchy) according to Locke's state of nature? What would Locke do in this situation?

Jean-Jacques Rousseau

Rousseau was a lone-wolf philosopher because he was very critical of the other philosophers and their theories. Rousseau believed that the reason philosophers were seen as so different and unrelatable was because they isolated themselves from the people who would read their philosophies so they could work in peace. Naturally, he thought this was an issue for political philosophers because they had to be trusted by the government to spread their theories. Rousseau argued philosophers (through governments and the court) put an emphasis on compassion and emotions instead of focusing on people's impulses.

Rousseau thought that people's feelings often make them act more kind than they really are because he thought kindness isn't really important when people are living in the state of nature. If you act kinder than you are, you will leave the state of nature, and your feelings won't get in the way of other people's needs. What matters is being free, but you can't be truly free if your feelings control you instead of your thoughts. At the same time, Rousseau said that true freedom can't happen if it means only doing what other people want because freedom is connected to who you are.

If your identity is linked to what other people need, you can lose your identity if those around you don't get what they need, which is a problem. Rousseau argued that it was the state's (government) responsibility to ensure the people kept their freedom and identity. To ensure this, he had a few political avenues to ensure the government and people knew how to preserve their freedom and identity.

There was a focus on public institutions like schools, libraries, and the police to encourage freedom and identity in people's daily interactions. The second avenue involved children and their developmental years (from babies to eight years old). The parents of these children were encouraged to teach their children about what freedom is and why their identity is so important. Rousseau believed this helped fight against later childhood behaviors like selfishness and cruelty.

Rousseau's form of the state of nature is vastly different from that of the other two political philosophers because he focused on encompassing the safety of freedom and autonomy from a young age without assuming adults would know what freedom and identity are. This unique state of nature rejected governments with representation (a government where members of the public have a say in political matters), and his version of the state of nature is self-rule.

He argued that any other form of government or state of nature would result in the slavery of the citizens, and they wouldn't be able to leave the state of nature if they wanted to. If the ruling party of the government lost favor with the people, the result would be a general decline in ethics and morality, and there would be less incentive for the citizens to behave morally.

Unlike the other two political philosophers, Rousseau was against the Christian church and their religious leaders because the church didn't encourage unity among the members, only separation based on how religious the church-goers were. He argued that the church or the government, if it was a religious government, couldn't protect its citizens from wrongdoing based only on faith. Rousseau's state of nature relied on the importance of education and self-rule, and he stated that the church could remove the state of nature by separating from the people who needed to form the state of nature in the first place.

If you followed Rousseau's state of nature, you would have to live with the knowledge that your parents aren't protected by the government. Do you think this will change how you view political philosophy?

Keep Thinking! Suggested Questions

Remember, there are no wrong answers to philosophical questions!

- What is an opinion?

- What is a human being?

- What are principles?

- What do you understand by the word "consent?"

Chapter 5:

Philosophy and Reality: How Do We Know What Is Real and What Is Not?

What Is Knowledge?

Knowledge is only possible by separating it from asking questions, allowing us to understand the "how" and "why" of what we know. Epistemology, the study of understanding knowledge, helps us understand historical topics and how we know something exists from what we experience through our associations. Propositional knowledge is another example of epistemology—it explains how general knowledge is linked to what we know based on what we have experienced ourselves. Propositional knowledge is also about understanding information according to the four paths to knowledge—belief, truth, justification, and memory. A priori knowledge, obtained from logic and reason, includes ethical reasoning, like knowing stealing is wrong. Understanding what is wrong in propositional knowledge is crucial for addressing issues like family and the law. By separating knowledge from questions, we can better understand the meaning of "how" and the extent of our knowledge.

Philosophy Can Be Personal

Let's look at this from a personal perspective: If you believe fairies exist because you see them in your mind, this adds to the knowledge you have about the world. By asking people if they believe in fairies and combining that knowledge with yours, you will know if fairies exist or not because of what you and others believe. At the end of the day, what you believe will change how you understand the world. If you believe fairies exist because others told you they have also seen them, you might not want to step on a patch of moss because fairies might live there. If you don't believe fairies exist, you probably won't mind stepping on the moss.

Belief is sometimes linked to truth. If you believe something is true, like the grass is green and the sky is blue, you have to believe there are colors called green and blue. Facts also add to how knowledgeable you are about the colors, grass, and the sky, which links facts and truth. In this case, truth is a conditional belief: If you have been taught that the sky is blue and the grass is green, you believe this is true, which adds to your knowledge about the world around you. Truth as a form of knowledge is only true if the facts (the grass is green and the sky is blue) add to how you understand the world around you.

Justification continues from truth and adds to your belief. For example, if you have a bedtime but you went to bed later than you were supposed to, your justification might be that you were reading a really good book and you didn't realize it was so late. Justification is obtained through evidence: The evidence that you stayed up past your bedtime is a book without a bookmark, for example. The book without a bookmark is real (justified) because everyone can see it. This adds to the knowledge you have of the world around you. Your parents knew you stayed up late. The next time you read past your bedtime, you might change your behavior to change what knowledge your parents or guardians have about your routine.

Memory is the final form of knowledge in this book, and you can use your memory to add to what you know. Memory also affects those around you because you have experienced it yourself. For example, if you walk in a puddle of water at school and your teacher complains you got the floor wet, the next time you think about the puddle might be when your friend is going to do the same thing. You could use your memory from when that happened to you to teach them that they could get into trouble. You will also be adding to your friend's knowledge because now they will know what your teacher likes and doesn't like.

What Is Reality?

Reality is our perception of the world and our understanding of what is important to us. It's influenced by our experiences at home and school and our actions that impact others. Philosophy focuses on reality through metaphysics and science, where we study the changes in our perception of the world from physical objects. Metaphysicists like David Hume and René Descartes argue that all materials used in science and math are real because they can confirm or deny the reality of something else. For example, a compass can indicate magnetism because it points to poles with a strong magnetic pull. Religious philosophers believe that objects and people on Earth are real because they are created by God or Allah.

Hume and the Empiricists

David Hume is considered the first empiricist because he focused on the differences between experience, imagination, and perception. Empiricism is the theory that all knowledge is derived from our sensory experiences. Perception deals with what should exist based on your surroundings, which includes the examples of religious philosophers. The perception that God or Allah gave their followers knowledge instead of their followers gaining knowledge through the perception of their own world is one way Hume explained religious experience, even though he wasn't a religious philosopher. He understood that different forms of knowledge needed the same experience and reasoning as other forms of philosophy.

Imagination, according to Hume, is also a form of reality. With your imagination, you can picture what a perfect world looks like. If you want a good world, you might try to act in ways that help make that picture of goodness come true. If knowledge comes from your imagination, then ideas you can't picture easily from your experiences can't help shape your reality.

Let's talk about this: If you can easily imagine or remember an experience you've had in nature, like a camping trip with stars in the sky that seem to go on forever, you will know there are more stars in the sky than you can see in the city. This adds to your experience of nature and the stars. If you only live in the city and never experience the night sky filled with so many stars that they light up the ground, you won't know this happens because you haven't experienced it.

Our Matter of Experience

Our experiences, according to Hume, come in two categories:

- Matter of fact: Experiences are like stories that connect ideas. They help us understand things and lead to more questions. When we learn and ask questions, it helps us in the future. Our experiences help us see what is real.

- Cause and effect: This happens when an idea or connection (like how a compass works with magnetic poles) shows how our experiences affect what we believe is real.

For example, the magnetic poles don't move to follow the compass, so the "matter" is the compass, and the "fact" is the poles. The fact of reality doesn't change based on the magnetic poles that don't move. The matter of reality is the needles in the compass, making up the matter or substance (just a fancy way of saying "stuff") of reality based on our understanding of how the compass works.

The Empiricism Arguments

A deduction is when the knowledge we have comes from separating the parts of what we know to understand each part separately before putting them back together. Intuition is when we understand something without needing to test the theory or separate the parts. If you followed a deductive argument about the reality of a plant, you would look at each leaf, the stem, the petals, the roots, the reproductive parts, and the soil. If all of those parts made a flower when put together, you can safely say the flower is real based on your deduction. If you saw the flower and just believed it was real because you know what a flower should look like, the flower would also be real, but from an intuition perspective.

Hume argued that deductive empiricism was important for reality because it's based on experiences. He also stated that your senses (that send your brain information about your experiences) are unreliable compared to using multiple proofs of reality, such as Thomas Hobbes's use of the state of nature to prove reality based on how people perceive their state of nature. Using your senses depends on different things, like your feelings that help you pay attention to something special or your situation, which can make you question what is real.

For example, if you feel sad because you just got some bad news, you might not realize that it's a sunny day. If you don't notice the sun because you are focused on your own thoughts and emotions, the sun's rays don't exist for you at the time, and your reality will change, even for a little while, because you deduce the sun's rays don't affect you.

Intuition and empiricism rely on memory and perception because intuition is only reliable if people need an answer to the question of reality itself without separating all the parts. It's very difficult to separate (deduce) all the parts of reality because no one seems to know what reality is. By putting your memories and experiences into perspective, you can understand what reality is by focusing on the argument as a whole. Think about it: If you go camping and you see the sky full of stars, you will understand there are millions of stars in the sky without needing to pick each one out of the sky and deduce that this one star makes up the galaxy alongside the other stars (deductions).

Descartes and the Rationalists

Rationalism is a unique form of philosophy because it focuses on two important philosophical arguments:

- Epistemology: This focuses on the theory of knowledge and how facts can be justified without opinion (almost the opposite of intuition)

- Objectivity: Focuses on the facts of an argument without opinion or past experiences influencing how the argument is understood.

For example, an epistemological argument might be how often your school lunches focus on healthy food and water instead of fast food and soda. The theory of the benefits of healthy food compared to fast food is part of the lunch team's knowledge without asking the students their opinion on what type of lunch they want. The objective thing to do when discussing lunch options is to ignore the opinions of the students and also ignore the type of popular food from the past.

Knowledge through experience is replaced by rational thinking and how an argument might sound if we use our intellect and logic instead of our experiences. Rationalism focuses on human nature because human nature leads you to do what is expected based on the (logical) outcome. When you ask questions about what it means to be human and stay safe, the smart answer is to think about the parts of being human that help us make good choices and keep us safe in real life.

Let's talk about this: A logical/rational outcome is an outcome that makes sense for those involved. A logical outcome to human nature would be people living according to their humanity instead of giving into their natural urges and falling into the state of nature where they might lose their individuality and autonomy.

If something can't be experienced to teach us how to think of it logically, the rationalists argue that it's not part of your reality. Things like death and birth aren't experiences you have had yet. Rationalism is a form of reality that only exists in your mind because of your experiences.

If you use your senses to form these experiences (or remember them), your senses are also real, but only if you can prove that they contribute to your reality. If, for example, you see a tree out your window during the day, your eyes contribute to your reality by adding a tree to the things you saw that day. If you look out your window at night and can't see the tree, what your eyes see doesn't contribute to your reality (because your reality is different during the day), so you shouldn't trust them.

The Power of Understanding

Descartes claimed that rationalism focused on a deeper understanding, and you can only understand something if you doubt it existed. However, through rational thinking, you understand and acknowledge what your original thought was. In true rationalist fashion, Descartes decided to doubt everything he knew and start from scratch, rationalizing why he believed what he thought he believed and why he saw what he thought he saw. Descartes started rationalizing his dreams and asked how he knew he wasn't dreaming when he was awake and awake when he was dreaming. He argues that even in his dreams, the formulas for math and science were still the same, so they were definitely real. That was his first proof of reality.

The second proof of reality is the question of "I" (him as a person). He rationalized that since he can doubt he exists as a person, he is real. If he wasn't real, he wouldn't have been able to doubt his reality. That's a lot of reality for a single person! His third proof of reality is his proof of God. He argued that knowing about God must have come from somewhere, and since God is a rational being who doesn't lie, God and reality exist. God exists because how else would Descartes have thought of Him, and reality exists because God created reality for Descartes to ask these questions.

A final proof of reality for Descartes is the existence of the outside world. Descartes can imagine the outside world like he imagined God, so if God exists because he imagined Him, the outside world also exists. The outside world for Descartes wasn't the natural world outside his windows; Descartes rationalized the outside world as his body and limbs in relation to his mind, where his thoughts questioned reality.

Keep Thinking! Suggested Questions

Remember! There are no wrong answers to philosophical questions.

- What do you understand by "familiar knowledge?"

- What is evidence?

- What do your surroundings include?

- What is a component?

- What is an illusion?

- What is the difference between an idea and an illusion?

- What is a direct cause?

- What is matter?

- What is intuition?

- What does it mean when something is unreliable?

- What is perception?

- What is logic?

Chapter 6:

Philosophy and Morals: What Does

It Mean to Be Good?

The common good means everyone should help improve the lives of others. Local courts create laws to support this by using police, the judicial system, and medical workers to assist those in need. The common good should not have negative effects; it should benefit everyone. It involves actions based on welfare and high moral standards. For example, if there is a local group that provides meals for children who can't afford school lunches, they are contributing to the common good because food is essential for survival and community participation.

Stealing, lying, and not educating children hurt the people in the community. A common good includes actions that reduce suffering, teach people about independence, and help your community recover from disasters like tornadoes or tsunamis. Learning about charity from a young age is also important because it shows you your potential for honesty and a giving nature while taking away any fears you might have about homelessness and not getting enough food.

Honesty helps everyone feel safe and secure. When people are truthful, it shows they care about each other's needs. Trustworthy people make others more comfortable. For example, if students face consequences for lying about homework, others are less likely to lie, too. When teachers reward honest students with good grades, it encourages a positive school environment and influences future behavior.

A Community of Accomplishments

Doing a good deed makes you feel accomplished and encourages more good deeds, even if no one notices. A good deed is still valuable whether or not it is seen. If your good actions inspire others, the feeling of accomplishment can grow. When one person's good deed benefits the community, everyone can share in that success. Good deeds often relate to community goals, and it's up to the community to define what is considered good compared to harmful activities.

If, for example, there is a park near important government buildings, the government may hire local gardeners to keep it nice. This helps create a good impression for visitors and can improve the community's reputation. If the park looks bad, political meetings might move elsewhere, which could reduce the government's influence in the area. A well-maintained park reflects positively on both the community and its political leaders, benefiting everyone.

Georg Hegel: Morals vs. Ethics

Logic and morality were the same thing, according to Hegel. He argued morality needs a form of logic because, without logic and understanding, people won't know how to recognize moral (good) deeds. At the same time, Hegel also argued that logic is one of the only ways to understand human nature: People do things to protect their human nature; otherwise, they might fall into the state of nature. The only way to avoid this is to focus on morality and good deeds for the community that you can relate to and easily join when necessary.

If these actions help the community and are easy for everyone to do, then they are morally justifiable because they contribute to the common good through logic and reasoning. For example, a good deed in your community could be a local trash collection drive. Since trash will most likely be in easily accessible places, the logical thing to do would be to collect the trash in these places based on your and your family's morality around littering.

Hegel had three arguments to prove or deny the morally justifiable way of life for your community:

- Crime: Crime can be looked at from different angles. From a moral perspective (like what the philosophers from this chapter studied), crime includes theft, fraud, and trespassing. From a political perspective, more serious crimes like murder and assault are included. When the police get involved, crime includes things the lawbreaker didn't take responsibility for or blamed on someone who didn't do anything wrong. When crime and the police are involved, you get something called mutual morality. This is needed to make sure the community is safe from moral and political crimes others might commit for selfish reasons.

- Deception: Deception can be hard to recognize because it isn't as noticeable as crime. Its effects on the community and government, where possible, last longer and affect more people than the consequences of crimes. Actions like the government lying to a community about how much food they need for the week or how much medicine is available in the hospitals have long-lasting and sometimes dangerous effects. We are more easily deceived by our friends and family who are close to us because it's easier for them to lie to us (they spend more time with us, so there are more opportunities). They may think it's acceptable to tell small lies, believing they won't get caught, but we usually notice and find the tricks people use.

- Punishment: Punishment and property are very similar, and most philosophers use both words at the same time. Property isn't just physical things like houses or cars; it can also include items that reflect your identity, like clothes, ID cards, or jewelry. Being able to make decisions for yourself (autonomy) is important for buying property and punishing those who take away your property, like a toy or your school books. Political items, like party banners, also count as property that shows your beliefs. This type of property is harder to take away because it's linked to your morals. Punishing someone for their beliefs is difficult because people who hold strong morals often resist being proven wrong.

- Property: Philosophical property includes your beliefs about right and wrong or politics. It's harder to take this away from you compared to physical possessions like a car or house because it's connected to your values. Punishing someone for their beliefs is tough since you can't punish them for having morals. People who care about their morals often struggle to accept being wrong, making it hard to punish them.

Let's think about all of the above like this: If you commit a moral crime, your friends and family might not want you to join their community because they won't feel safe around you. If you go into an off-limits area and the owner of the property confronts you for trespassing, you could accuse them of harassment because you didn't want to be disturbed while exploring. When you transfer the blame from yourself to an innocent person (the owner of the property in this case), a moral crime is committed because you take away their ability to make decisions based on what they believe is right for themselves and their land.

If you deceive (lie to) someone you know, a logical reaction they have could be they will stop telling you things about themselves and their lives. If people you know start realizing you have deceived them, they might all stop giving you information about what's important in the community and in their lives. They could assume that you have different morals and values, and they might want to focus on those in the community who share their morals so they can share common interests. This will make it very difficult for you to form relationships and stay in the community because you will become a social outcast. No one will trust you, and people you knew from childhood might start avoiding you altogether.

An example of punishment and property from a moral view could be when different family members disagree about political parties. If your aunt puts up banners for the party she follows, your parents, who support the other party, might feel upset for speaking out against your aunt's opinion. Your parents might be more open to other opinions and show support in quieter ways (by not having a banner in the living room), so when they share their different beliefs, your aunt might feel offended because your parents don't agree with her choice. The way people think about right and wrong depends on what others believe. According to Hegel, living in a way that makes sense morally is more complicated than just being in the same place together.

Practicing Ethics

For Hegel, there are two types of morality:

- Inward morality: This is your personal morality, and these morals are directly related to our family, education, and, in most cases, our religious background (or no religious background if our families aren't religious), and it's what we do with these morals that translates into ethics. Intrinsic literally means inward, so the morality you have according to what you believe from your inner circle (family) is also called inward morality.

- Outward morality: This is about how you can be free in your town and with the people around you. When you learn about being good and kind outside your home, it helps you know how to act when you're with others. Outward morality relates to what your community thinks is right or wrong, and it also shows everyone how to be good. These important lessons can include being kind, sharing, and helping people who need it.

Let's look at it like this: Let's say morality is the wind. Unless the wind blows, the trees and flowers won't move because the trees and flowers aren't influenced by the wind. If ethics are the trees and flowers you see, you will be able to see the effect of the wind on them—they don't exist separately.

Hegel argued there is a difference between morals and ethics because he believed ethics can't be taught; they are the result of a learned belief system from within your family and, as you age, from your surrounding community. Ethics is related to how we behave in the community based on what type of morality we were taught as children.

A good example of someone living a moral-rich life while doing ethical things is the concept of kindness. If your family is kind from a moral perspective and they believe all insects and animals deserve to live, the ethical practice you might focus on is stepping over insects on the sidewalk to protect them instead of squishing them because "they are just stupid insects."

John Stuart Mill: Who Is Responsible for Morality?

Mill was a political and moral philosopher who believed the state and government have a moral obligation to the liberties and rights of the citizens. He argued that anything that infringes on someone's rights or opportunities to participate in their community is immoral and should be avoided at all costs. Examples of these include jail, any activity that forbids citizens from participating in the economy, such as opening a business or employing people to work on your property, and activities that don't contribute to the general good of the state. In that case, Mill's moral and political philosophy is a combined effort to benefit everyone instead of the individual morality prioritized by Hegel.

In Mill's moral politics, it's society's job to stop bad actions to make a good community, but society only knows what immoral acts are because of its chosen government. At the same time, Mill believed that people should care more about doing the right thing than just listening to the government. The government should help teach everyone about their rights and what is morally right so they can choose the kind of government they want. He explains morality falls into two categories: "weak moralism" and "strong moralism" (Brink, 2007).

Weak moralism can only be protected by the government if there are separate groups of people who follow lesser-known moralities that are not widely practiced. In this case, the government can protect its morality by focusing on the groups that have less of a moral claim to an idea compared to strong moralism, where general acceptance from the group is needed to survive without government intervention.

Let's discuss this: If your community consists of small groups of people, each with their own idea of what morality is and each in conflict with one another, your rights as a community could be lessened because of a lack of a common goal. For example, if you and your family (group one) believe it's your moral obligation to celebrate and say goodbye to your deceased loved ones at sea, but your neighbors (group two) think this is wrong, they could try removing your autonomy about this decision by getting the government involved. The government will have to hear both sides of the moral argument and make a decision based on personal accounts. This is weak moralism.

If your family believes in the moral obligation of the sea celebrations for your loved one, they could ask their neighbors for help if they believe this would add to the moral community. If the neighbors help, both families practice strong moralism because they settle their moral obligations as a unit without the government getting involved. After all, the morality practiced by your family was accepted. According to Mill's moral theory, the government should know about the different types of morality and people in their state, but they aren't required to get involved unless asked. Strong moralism is often seen as a form of welfare because morality and personal liberties aren't questioned when strong moralism is practiced for the benefit of all.

Freedom, Liberties, and Morality

To have freedom and liberty, the government is responsible for fighting for your morality as a common good. Mill believed morality was an opportunity for citizens to focus on personal freedoms like their choice of partner, job, and hobby, based on their moral compass. The opposite could happen if these needs aren't met, and they would instead justify their safety (freedom from harm) by participating in crime to protect their freedoms. In this case, the citizens will have a reduced trust in the government, and this could lead to charity. Mill argued charity is immoral because it encourages dependence on others instead of focusing on your own life and liberties, robbing you of the freedom to choose for yourself.

Morality depends a lot on individualism. If the community's sense of right and wrong helps everyone, the government will keep its promise to focus on people's freedoms and chances to learn about morality. Let's look at it like this: If you live in a country where your rights (liberties) are protected because the moral compass of the government aligns with your family's moral compass, your family will be free to choose political parties, religion, areas you live in, and the friends you keep because this aligns with the government's expectation of your moral compass. If your family takes liberties away from people in their community by not allowing them to work in a specific role or wear certain clothes because your family doesn't agree with their morality, the government, according to Mill, has the right to restrict your family's freedom because you are restricting another's freedom.

Immanuel Kant: Virtue is Doing Your Duty

Kant believed that it's our job to seek examples of morality and behave accordingly. He argued that to understand goodwill and a good deed, the foundation for making moral choices is important. Internal morality isn't something everyone understands, and it's the job of the people (not the government) to push for a moral purpose in their community. This will allow them to reflect on their life and how their life has affected those around them.

Let me explain: If you help someone in need because you feel it's the right thing to do, your kindness affects their life. They might think about something they did for you before that made you want to help. You can also think back on your own actions to understand your future: Will it be filled with helping others and thankful people, or will it be filled with people you could have helped but decided not to?

Kant thought it was important for everyone to be responsible and try their best to do what is right for themselves and their community. If you don't do your best, it wouldn't be fair because you wouldn't be being honest with yourself. Kant believed that lying and tricking others is bad because it makes it hard for people to trust each other about what is right and wrong.

The Moral Compass

Kant's moral compass revolved around beliefs and sayings that the community members focused on, and he argued these were directly related to the moral compass of the community. For example, "a person with good will" is taken as an indicator of the moral compass because it focuses on morality and autonomy from different angles. The word "person" represents autonomy, while "goodwill" represents intent (a desire to do something), which is related to morality because it's your moral compass that drives your actions and desires.

If you say something like, "I'm sure they meant well," when reflecting on the actions of someone else, you are participating in Kant's moral compass example. Let me explain: The words "I'm" and "they" represent autonomy because they both relate to something about people. "Sure," "meant," and "well" all represent morality because to be sure of something, you have to believe it is true. A belief system is part of morality, and to mean something is to intend for something specific to happen. Wishing someone well is also connected to morality because your feelings about right and wrong influence whether you want to help someone in need or not.

Keep Thinking! Suggested Questions

Remember, there are no wrong answers to philosophical questions!

- What is a common good?

- What job do the courts have?

- What is an opportunity?

- What do you understand by "untrustworthy?"

- What is an accomplishment?

- What is good for a community?

- What do you understand by the word "trapped?"

- What is a benefit?

- What are freedoms?

- What is a duty?

- What does "they mean well" mean?

- What are controlled actions?

- What is freedom?

Chapter 7:

The Eastern Thinkers: Lao Tzu and Confucius

Chinese vs. Eastern Philosophy

Eastern philosophy is a broad term used to describe the thoughts and wisdom of East Asian countries. These countries include:

- China

- Japan

- India

- Korea (before it was split into North and South Korea)

- Vietnam

Each of these countries had its own version of Eastern philosophy because of the important people who passed through them at the time, teaching their philosophy. These people include:

- Lau-Tzu and Confucius from China (spoken about in this chapter).

- Siddhartha Gautama (the Buddha) (spoken about in the next chapter).

Since Eastern philosophy covers so many countries and groups of people, it's a combination of different ways of thinking throughout the region. It includes Confucianism and Taoism, plus the theories and philosophies brought over by the Western settlers before China, Japan, India, Korea, and Vietnam had their modern borders.

In Eastern philosophy, there isn't only one argument to try and explain what rationality is like there is in the West. The Eastern philosophers and governments combined all the teachings of reality, rationality, and morality as a way of life instead of something to be studied in a classroom.

Because of this, Chinese philosophy includes important movements from the West like sophism (from Descartes) and legalism (from Mill), which are forms of government that focus on morality and the law, as well as the ancient Chinese customs from the important dynasty or family at the time.

Mohism is a form of Chinese philosophy, and it was a style of government and community that was similar to Greece's style of science and debate. Introduced by Mo Di, Neo-Mohism is the modern form of Mohism, and Chinese philosophers thought this was necessary to address modern issues such as international treaties. Ancient China didn't have any treaties because the ruling parties were the important families, and relationships with other countries were not necessary. There was also something called Yin-Yang interactionism, which focused on balancing good and bad forces in society. You can probably spot the Yin-Yang symbol around your town, maybe on the side of a Chinese restaurant or if you walk past a tattoo parlor with pictures in the windows.

Mohism and Yin-Yang interactionism were important philosophies that contributed to the development of medieval China. The medieval period sparked an educational and industrial boom that made China significant globally. As a result, the government needed a mix of old and new ideas for its educated population. Chinese philosophy explored topics like logic, math, science, and biology while emphasizing history.

Think about it: If you have a school project for English and your teacher asked you to look into Shakespeare, would you only focus on the well-known plays like Romeo and Juliet or Hamlet, or would you include his early works like King Henry VI? By looking at his early works, you will have an understanding of how Shakespeare used language to get his message across regardless of his audience.

In the same way, studying Chinese philosophy helps us understand China's history and politics in a simpler way than Western philosophy. It allows for new ideas to emerge for the benefit of your community instead of people in the government, which is how a lot of governments practice politics today. Modern Chinese philosophy merges philosophy, politics, and government into one view, using ancient ideas to guide the future and understand the past. It feels more like a political agreement than a lifestyle compared to Eastern philosophy.

When Buddhism came to China, it spread quickly despite the imperial family's focus on promoting earlier teachings of the dynasty. The Chinese government didn't allow people to have different ideas or religions than the government believed in, and the people were encouraged instead to focus on science, logic, and math in education. They believed that the Buddha lost his influence after reaching enlightenment and didn't fit into their philosophies, which prioritized rational thought.

Think about it: If the next town over had a religious focus while your town had a focus on biology, politicians who need to campaign in both towns would need to consider both ways of life to make sure they get their message across. If your community started putting posters up comparing your town with the neighboring town, politicians who read the posters would think about the pros and cons of both towns instead of only your town. This would help them choose the right form of campaigning and government for their personal philosophies and way of life.

Teaching Eastern Philosophy

Eastern philosophy is very different from Chinese philosophy because it includes the teachings of Buddhism, Hinduism, and Shintoism from a mystical perspective without the politics involved. In Eastern philosophy, there is a big focus on the quality of life and the quality of the people without too much focus on the politics and economics of the land. In Chinese philosophy, philosophies are less scientific, which gives Eastern philosophy more room to grow as distinct philosophies (Buddhism and Shintoism) without any outside influence.

To understand Eastern philosophy, we must look at the important qualities that shape Eastern philosophy and what separates it from Chinese philosophy. Negative thoughts are welcomed in Eastern philosophy because this allows you to come to a helpful conclusion yourself or sometimes with the help of the kami, who are divine spirits who act as messengers and healers of the home and garden around you. Understanding yourself and your place in the world is important for Eastern philosophy. This is only possible when you understand the personal limitations of your mind, the physical limitations of your body, the concept of death and sickness, and your ability to be good despite the forces that try to lead you astray (the kami). Most kami are good and want to help you and your family in the home or garden, but there are also bad kami, called impurity kami, which are discussed in the next chapter.

Think about it: If you are worried about a test or a social event where you don't know anyone and you spend a night worrying, you could ask yourself why you feel like this. If you consider your place in the test or your social circle before you go to the event, you will gain an understanding of what might be expected of you. The stress (limitations) you feel won't be as severe as you thought they might be, and you'll be able to contribute to the grade or your social circle with a clear mind.

Similarly to the life and death cycle the Buddha went through after his enlightenment, everything is connected to everything else in Eastern philosophy. There wasn't a "beginning" of the world, and there won't be an end. The myths about the birth of Japan and China don't mean the world had a beginning: The Earth (the world) was already there when Japan and China were formed; they were just formed by the kami. There isn't a beginning or end because everything is a part of nature, and in nature, death isn't really death. The plants and animals who die give life to the plants and animals around them, completing the circle of life, like an Eastern form of *The Lion King*. Eastern philosophy from a Buddhist perspective focuses on life, death, and regeneration, while from the

Shintoism perspective, there is a focus on the kami and the importance of nature in our daily lives.

The Important Healers

Lao-Tzu: Generosity and Selflessness in a Person

Lau-Tzu, also known as Lau-Tzi or Laozi, was a Chinese philosopher who focused on contemplation and virtue. Lau-Tzu wasn't his actual name but a title given by his contemporaries because of his patience and wisdom. No one knows what his actual name was, but many Chinese scholars thought Lau-Tzu was a childhood nickname that he used as an adult because so many people knew him by that name already. On the other hand, some scholars have argued he didn't live at all, which gives us a glimpse of his naming style: Those who named him needed virtue and peace in their lives, and they found someone to embody this. The people who needed his wisdom named him according to their needs. If you have a pet, how did you name them? Did you name them Courage because that's what you needed, or did you name them Butch because you needed a big scary dog to scare the birds away from your parent's vegetable garden? For the scholars who believed he existed, Lau-Tzu was seen as the connecting force between happiness, fulfillment, and creativity.

This potentially imagined philosopher believed the Tao (how we live our lives and decide what is good or bad in a way that feels natural, also called natural morality) existed, and its flow was a mystical water that healed those it touched and brought clarity and peace. Lao-Tzu believed people should embrace the Tao because this was how they could prove their goodness. The Taoist philosophy includes a deep respect for the natural world, the sharing of ancient intellectual ideas about ethics, the defense of individual liberties, and the idea of natural morality. As is common in Eastern philosophy, Lao-Tzu believed people are naturally good. The reason they did something wrong is that the government is not working well, and the laws are not good. The only way people can rid themselves of the opportunity to be bad is through education and understanding.

The alternative is that people don't realize their own potential, which takes them further away from the Tao.

Think about this: The Tao is a great snake slithering across the grass. When you go near it, it could coil away because it doesn't know you. As you and the Tao snake get to know one another, you become more comfortable with each other, and you step closer. The Tao snake also recognizes you, so it welcomes you in its presence. As the Tao snake moves through the grass, you follow it, and you get to experience what it sees. You experience the sun on your face, the different colored flowers, and the insects and animals that live in the grass, and you get to see how the Tao snake moves, so you feel safe around it.

If your friends see you following a snake, they might question you, but once you explain the wonders you have seen, they will join you and the Tao snake in the grass, understanding the nature of the world through its eyes and tongue. If your friend disagrees with something you have said, they might leave the side of the Tao snake, leaving the understanding of the grass and forest behind. This is the nature of Taoism from the teachings of Lau-Tzu: Focus on instinct (of the Tao snake) over intellect (disagreements), and you won't need to leave the Tao's presence.

The philosophers and historians who believed he didn't exist argued that he was the representation of wisdom related to old age and that he was a sage of respect and understanding. A sage is a Chinese term for elderly teachers, and the word respect usually accompanies the title. Lau-Tzu was respected as a mythical and physical teacher, and many argue he was Confucius's first teacher (if he did, in fact, exist).

Confucius: Medicine Man, Psychologist, and Healer

Combining myths and legends with reality was the norm for Chinese philosophers, and this was no different for Confucius. Confucius was the name given to him by the West when his philosophies became known worldwide. His true name is a combination of his name and the title he had. Kong Qui was his given name and Confucius was seen as a title mixed with his name, meaning Master. The historical representation of Confucius is connected to Chinese myths and legends linked to his time of birth and the abilities his parents believed he had.

Even with the mythical component, his existence wasn't questioned, and he became the most prominent Chinese philosopher in the East and West. Many of his policies are still in place in Chinese politics, and historians in the West study his methods to gain a better understanding of Chinese philosophy and customs. He was highly educated, and when he was old enough, he was introduced to the administrative powers of the Chinese bureaucracy. He prided himself on linking ancient Chinese customs to the modern world to keep the old history important and interesting.

These customs were to please the Chinese deities and educate the imperial family regarding matters of the state and the influence of nature spirits for the benefit of the people. In his teachings, he tried to strengthen the idea that it's important to understand the world around you before trying to understand the political world. These teachings came at a perfect time because the dynasty in practice before Confucianism was the Qin dynasty. They favored money over people, which is what Confucius fought against.

In the Qin dynasty, there was a shift from family and nature to business and profit, and at the time, people saw Confucius as a vital part of Chinese history and culture while lacking the ability to modernize China to compete in the world market. Confucius's ideas were, in many ways, the founding principles of the imperial politics and economics sectors. He was out of touch with modern issues, and the younger politicians saw this as a threat to their global influence. Confucius's popularity coincided with the new Han dynasty, which chose Confucianism as the state religion and ideology.

Think about this: When you were very little, the way your parents spoke to you was probably different compared to how they speak to you now. There wasn't anything wrong with how they spoke to you as a very young child; your worldview and comprehension were just different. For example, if you struggled to say the word "supper," your parents might have said "sup" when they told you it was supper time so you could understand what they meant. As an older child, you can probably say "supper," and the way your parents say "sup" might sound odd to you.

You have outgrown the word "sup," and if they keep saying that, it might sound weird and lose its meaning. This is what the younger generation of Chinese people thought about Confucius.

Taoism as a Religion

Taoism was developed as a religion first because of Lao-Tzu's teachings and what he believed in—appreciating and worshiping nature—instead of a philosophy because modern philosophy is understood as a way to process information and discuss what is said. We understand Taoism as a philosophy now because of the debates and discussions between Taoist leaders and their people to understand a specific way of life. The Tao way of life was nature worship and the sharing of ancient philosophical concepts regarding ethics, the protection of personal freedoms, and the concept of natural morality—a philosophical discussion around kindness to nature and those who benefit from its resources.

In Taoism, the main source of ethics and morality (both very important concepts in philosophy) comes from a philosophy of protection of all living things. Theft, deception, and unnecessary harm (killing without needing to for survival) can be removed if you follow the Tao and listen to how the Tao way of life can guide you towards good behavior without anyone else telling you right from wrong.

Confucianism as a Religion

In a similar way to Taoism, Confucianism was considered a religion before a philosophy, but this changed when the writings about Confucius were discovered, and the scholars of the modern world were able to read his doctrines focused on logic, morality, and autonomy. Confucius didn't believe in gods or kami, which was very unusual for his time. He focused on ancestor worship and the importance of the family. He placed great emphasis on education and community, which he used as practices in Confucianism. Meditations on how to live a good life are a central part of Confucianism, and the distinction between good and bad moral character fuels his main philosophy of "cosmic harmony" (The Wise Apple, n.d.).

In Confucianism, everything is linked to balance and harmony, and the rituals performed then and now are intended to encourage a positive attitude and respect for yourself and your community. There is a lot of respect for the elderly in Confucianism, and many Chinese scholars use this as proof that Lao-Tzu was a real person and that he taught Confucius. Confucianism was the state religion of China from 202 B.C.E. to 1912, but it shared a spot with Buddhism and Taoism. As a result of globalization, China moved away from these religions and philosophies in favor of more modern religions like Christianity and Islam, which is exactly what Confucius was scared of.

Keep Thinking! Suggested Questions

Remember! There are no wrong answers to philosophical questions.

- What is a philosophical movement?

- What is a historical component?

- What is an improved life?

- What is a comparison?

- What is happiness?

- What is a faulty law?

- What is a social issue?

- What is a political issue?

- What is a balanced life?

Chapter 8:

Buddhism and Shintoism: The Life

Spirits

What Is Buddhism?

Buddhism started with who we now know as the Buddha, but that wasn't his real name. In India (where he came from), he was named Shakyamuni, and in the West, he was called Siddhartha Gautama. Like many Eastern philosophies and religions, the tales around his life combine stories and mythologies of his life. The stories written about him in the palace are considered history because there are palace records and scribes who wrote about Shakyamuni. His father was an influential person, and he had to document everything that happened in his palace and domain to show his people he wasn't using the money from taxes for personal gain.

Once Shakyamuni left the palace and focused on his enlightenment, the historical stories from the palace changed into myth. This makes it very difficult to separate facts from stories people tell, which adds to the wonder and spiritual nature of the religion. Even so, the details about his life are important because they paved the way for his philosophical journey and eventual enlightenment. His life and story started in a palace, like all good adventures!

In Buddhism, enlightenment happens when you are reborn after you die so you can make better choices in your new life. Shakyamuni, an important figure in Buddhism, could remember the lives he lived before being born into a palace and a luxurious life. We don't know what those past lives were because there are no writings about them, but we can guess that they helped him become a better person each time he was born and died, leading to his enlightenment. When he became enlightened, all his past experiences helped him become a better Buddha because he was more confident and understood right from wrong.

Shakyamuni was part of a noble family and was highly educated in the palace where he was born because he wasn't allowed to leave the house. Some historians say this is where his journey took root: A curiosity to experience the outside world. Even as an adult, his actions were controlled, and in a way, this fueled his questioning fire. At 29 years old, he was allowed to leave the palace four times a year, and he used these trips to learn as much of the outside world as possible. He called these journeys his "sights" because, during each outing, he saw something that shaped the way he saw the world. These lessons became the backbone of Buddhism when he started educating people about his way of life.

Think about it like this: If you leave town for a school trip and the area you travel to for the day is at the coast while your home is inland, you might compare the houses and the people and think about how each area can offer something different. You might compare how the windows of the coastal towns have bars on them compared to the windows at home. The bars aren't for security reasons: Coastal towns and cities are often very humid, and this weather attracts small monkeys to nest in the palm or beach trees. At home, there won't be any bars on the windows because your family isn't afraid of monkeys coming in and eating your fruit from the bowl on the table. For Shakyamuni, what he saw on his trips was very different from his life in the palace, and it affected him deeply.

The first "sight" he had was an old man, unable to move properly because of his age. The second "sight" was a sick person, unable to heal themselves properly because they didn't have the right medicine. Death was the third "sight" because Shakyamuni walked past a ditch in the road and saw a person who had recently passed away. The final (and for the sake of Buddhism, the most important) "sight" received by Shakyamuni was a monk on a quest to find the truth of his religion. The texts describing these events don't specify which religion the monk was trying to find the truth of. Based on the time and location (Ancient India), it could have been Hinduism. All of these "sights" put Shakyamuni on his own path to philosophical enlightenment, and he left the only home he had ever known to find the answers to these questions:

- Why do we age?

- What happens when our medicine isn't enough?

- Why do we die?

- Can we become enlightened (gain knowledge of all the important questions in life)?

Shakyamuni believed the path to enlightenment was through discipline and reflection. He called this asceticism, and it's still practiced today. To practice this type of control, he would fast (not eat or drink anything for a set amount of time), spend hours meditating about what was important, and push his body to the limit when it came to activities like farm work or helping others. After practicing this lifestyle for a while, he decided the extreme approach wasn't the way to enlightenment because he didn't achieve it.

At the time, the Bodhi tree was considered sacred because of its connection with joy and understanding. The leaves of the tree are heart-shaped, and the figs that come from it symbolize understanding because they were used to feed the hungry, like an ancient soup kitchen. The information about when Shakyamuni became the Buddha under the Bodhi tree isn't as elaborate as other philosophical texts because Shakyamuni was the only one there. People wrote hundreds of texts about him after he became the Buddha, but as Shakyamuni, he was just an ordinary man sitting under a tree, possibly eating a fig. Legend says that Shakyamuni achieved enlightenment under the sacred Bodhi tree after traveling throughout Ancient India for 45 years.

The Start of a Religion

Each piece of writing about the Buddha pieced together his life before and after his enlightenment. Buddha's disciples followed him around India to document his actions and share them with the world, no different from Western philosophy contemporaries following their masters to spread their wisdom. The different forms of Buddhism practiced in India and worldwide haven't strayed much from the path of enlightenment. The start of the religion was a philosophy that dealt with conservative teachings and respect for nature, known as Theravada Buddhism. This style of Buddhism follows the asceticism lifestyle practiced by the Buddha before his enlightenment and isn't as accepting as the later styles.

Theravada Buddhism is considered the closest way of life to what the Buddha experienced, according to his followers, and is considered the only form of Buddhism by people who want to uphold the ancient tradition. There are strict rules regarding behavior and diet, and these rules directly correlate to what Shakyamuni experienced before he became the Buddha. Those who follow Theravada Buddhism aren't allowed to handle money directly and have a money pouch or box for any transactions.

Theravada Buddhists can only eat food that they prepared themselves, including water, because of the hunger Shakyamuni felt when he chose not to eat any meat. If Shakyamuni wasn't able to safely prepare the meat from animals he met on the road, he couldn't eat it. It's much easier to prepare fruit and vegetables because all you need is a knife and a cutting board. Preparing meat is a lot more complicated. Theravada Buddhism focuses on hard work and doing the work yourself.

The first few years of searching for enlightenment were trying for Shakyamuni because he left a life of luxury, and those who follow Theravada Buddhism attempt to copy his actions as closely as possible so they can achieve enlightenment. Meditation and contemplation are also a vital part of Theravada Buddhism because of the days spent in meditation by Shakyamuni before and after his enlightenment. Through meditation, it's believed you can reflect on your good and bad deeds while focusing on your karma, which will help your own enlightenment.

These rules seem very strict, but they teach the Theravada Buddhists in a way the Buddha would have taught them if he were alive today. Think about it like this: At home, you probably have rules to keep you safe and out of trouble. By following these rules, your life improves because you have the discipline to follow them. If you have a bedtime, it means your parents want you to have a good night's sleep so you can concentrate on school the following day. The Theravada Buddhists use Buddha as the voice telling them to go to bed early so they can concentrate on their meditations in the morning.

As far as Eastern philosophy goes, Theravada Buddhism is the only form of Buddhism that qualifies as a philosophy. The other two forms of Buddhism—Mahayana and Vajrayana (also called Tibetan Buddhism)—are influenced by modern culture. This influence removes the philosophical aspects of Buddhism, such as the search for truth and wisdom (enlightenment) and the questioning nature of the four important questions Shakyamuni asked when he left the palace walls.

Buddhism: A Way of Life and Philosophy

The No Harm Rule

This rule focuses on compassion and patience. The Buddha believed all life is precious—even the insects on the ground—and Buddhists don't harm or kill insects or animals unless their life depends on it. The Buddhist philosophy encourages people to become vegetarians, and if you must eat meat, you should make sure the animal leads a good and healthy life before they die for food.

The Property Rule

Property for Buddhists includes all physical possessions like this book, your phone if you have one, and your school books. The property rule involves not taking more property than required. Let's look at it like this: If you have books at home, but you go to the library for more books without thinking about others who might need the books more than you do, you will break the property principle because you took more than you needed. In Buddhism, if you take more than you need, you disrespect the other person's property because they will have to take more than they need from another person, disrespecting their property and way of life.

The Dishonesty Rule

Lying is a form of dishonesty that hurts people around you because—at least in the Buddhist philosophy—you speak without adding any wisdom to the conversation. If you are dishonest, you won't know if the person you are speaking to feels comfortable around you. For Buddhists, this will break their enlightenment because it involves the no-harm rule as well since you harm people's trust when you lie to them.

The Intoxication Rule

Intoxication means to do something so often that it affects your life and those around you. Normally, people speak about alcohol when discussing intoxication, but Buddhism has a wider variety of intoxicating actions that can be applied to our lives. You can become intoxicated with the feeling you get when you watch your favorite TV show instead of sleeping because you just have to know what's coming next. Your life depends on knowing what happens next in *Hotel Transylvania*!

Internet chatrooms also have an intoxicating effect: If you are in a chatroom with someone who just "gets you," you might feel pressured to add them to your real-life friend group because you are intoxicated by the feeling that someone finally understands your personality. All of these forms of intoxication are what the Buddha warned people about.

When we are too focused on the feeling we get when something goes well, we sometimes forget to think about life outside the good or intoxicating feelings. Not everything has to feel like an exciting adventure. Think about the Buddha: He spent years meditating and reflecting on his life without going for the next intoxicating feeling, and we still speak about him today!

What is Shintoism?

Outside Buddhism, Shintoism is the main religion of Japan. Unlike Buddhism, Shintoism's influence isn't internationally well-known. In Shintoism, there is a focus on culture first and philosophy/religion second. It's considered by most Japanese people and historians of the East as a personal religion with a single focus.

A personal religion doesn't need a big religious building for all of the followers; it's a religion about you and what you think is important in nature and the world around you. The history of Shintoism is closely tied to the mythical (instead of historical) culture of Japan and the importance of the archipelago (a cluster of islands that makes up a geographical territory) and the noble families who lived there. The way Japanese imperialism (a way of government where an emperor is elected and rules over the people with absolute power) is linked to the lands in Shintoism follows ancient Japanese history where the archipelago was created by the mythical ancestors of the emperor who was put in charge of the islands after an important wedding of the kami.

Shintoism focuses on the land, soil, and all the plants and animals created when the islands were formed by two kami called Izanagi and Izanami. Although Shintoism didn't start out with religious books, Shinto texts grew when people shared their way of life with their families, mainly in the form of poetry.

Why Is Shintoism Popular?

Shintoism is popular because of the general belief that we are born good and have the potential to do good things for others without being told. This helps people understand their purpose in life: If you help others as a child because it makes you feel good and it helps you do something productive instead of spending the whole day watching a TV show, when you grow up, you might become a psychologist or social worker because you helped others as a child without being told to. If you or your family followed the Shintoism philosophy, you would appease the kami in your home because the kami would recognize you were born good and chose a career path to use your good attributes.

If you are allowed to read the news, you might notice the world is full of pain. Shintoism has a philosophy of "do no harm," just like Buddhism. Shintoism has gained popularity over the years because it's seen as a peaceful solution to address the uncertainty and negative influences of the world in general. Shintoism can calm our minds and help our conscience by focusing on the kami instead of the harm in front of us.

Shintoism: Are There Spirits in Philosophy?

The Kami Follow the Rules

The main belief in Shintoism focuses on divine spirits. These spirits aren't gods in the Christian or Islamic sense. They are messengers, healers, and keepers of the house and garden. The single focus of Shintoism philosophy is to gain wisdom by respecting nature. Kami are the spirits who guide us on our path. By appeasing nature (where the kami live), they will share their knowledge and wisdom with us. Each aspect of nature has a specific kami who represents it, and each natural side of our world (the trees, plants, rocks, animals, and insects) embodies the kami as a thank you for returning to living in harmony and peace with those on the property, or the people in parks and mountains across Japan.

If the kami are pleased, they grant blessings to the land and people who show them respect, and if you are lucky enough, the kami might show themselves in mirrors or reflections in your home. Let's think about it like this: If you have a kami in your home, it might be linked to the potted plant or water feature in the living room. The kami want to be near nature, so they will focus on the potted plants and water features because they might assume you made a shrine for them. The kami and Shintoism, in general, don't need elaborate buildings like the religious buildings found in the West, and they don't need high-ranking officials to become priests. Instead, they need nature, a Shinto priest that was taught by the priest before them, and an understanding that people are good.

Small Shinto shrines created by Shinto priests can be found anywhere in the Japanese landscape where the priests ask the kami for a blessing or guidance. These shrines are filled with various foods and items to entice the kami to come down to Earth. Each kami can descend onto a kami shrine, and when they do, they give the person who called for them Japanese wisdom passed down from the kami before them. The kami who visit the shrines also encourage the priests and important leaders who call for them to share their knowledge and wisdom about the kami and Shinto philosophy with anyone who will listen. Who knows, you might have a kami watching your house and garden because a Shinto priest asked them to spread their wisdom to your family!

What Causes People to Do Bad Things?

Since people who follow Shintoism believe we are born good, when people do bad things, it must be from an external source. This is where a new type of kami comes in: The impurity kami. In Shintoism, balance is everything, and when things are out of balance, it's the result of outside forces that cause people to sin. Sinning in Shintoism is when you give the kami a reason to stop protecting your home by being unkind to your visitors or when you stop respecting nature in your garden. If you sin like this, the kami will stop protecting you in your home by allowing cracks to appear in your walls (the kami usually fix the cracks if you are on good terms with them), or the kami could hurt your social standing because they feel neglected—if the kami misbehave in the garden, the flowers and grass will look unkempt, which could be embarrassing for the people who live there.

The impurity kami is also responsible for how people behave at a funeral. The quick end to someone's life force, which was a part of the natural world the kami protected, causes a lot of heartache and pain for the people in the family. The impurity/bad kami are responsible for how people behave in mourning since they aren't themselves. In Japan, family members who have lost a loved one don't have to follow the ordinarily strict rules in their community because their actions aren't their own. These rules can include punctuality, a certain dress code, or crying in public, which is seen as very rude in Japan. According to Shinto philosophy, people who do bad things are under the influence of the impurity kami, and they need to remove the kami before more damage is done.

Keep Thinking! Suggested Questions

Remember! There are no wrong answers to philosophical questions.

- What do you understand by the term "highly educated?"

- What is a legend?

- What are extremes?

- What is enlightenment?

- What is Karma?

- What is meditation?

- What is vegetarianism?

- What do you understand by the word "harm?"

- What makes something popular?

- What is a peaceful solution?

- What is mourning?

Chapter 9:

Contemporary Philosophy: Today's Burning Questions

Out With the Old, In With the New

Contemporary philosophy is a way to discuss modern issues with a combination of old and new philosophical ideas. For example, the current problem of how involved your country should be in your life and its influence on your decisions is an issue the ancient Romans felt regarding government intervention in their daily lives. Before the fall of the Roman empire, citizens had very strict rules on how they could dress in public and what goods they were allowed to buy. The Roman government believed they had the authority to control the spending habits of their people, which put their citizens in financial ruin because they were forced to buy expensive Roman goods. The result was an unhappy region with poor citizens.

Today, countries prioritize the betterment of their citizens, and governments are legally allowed to make decisions for their citizens if they think it's in people's best interests. In high-crime areas, the government can request more police or prisons to combat crime. The rights and autonomy of the person are taken away if they are a danger to society and don't contribute to the improvement of the community.

Historical events can create opportunities for modern philosophers to devise plans that help governments manage their people, economy, and political influence with a more hands-on approach. Contemporary philosophy is broken up into the following methods:

- Analytic philosophy is one part, and this is used to explain and teach philosophy in a way that is understandable to the general public by avoiding the use of technical terminology.

- Think about it like this: If I said, "The graminoids grew under the pontoon where the highbrow made their foremost philosophical unveiling," your reaction would probably be *I don't understand* or *What am I reading?* But if I said: "The grass grew under the bridge where the thinker made their first philosophical discovery," you would understand what I meant.

- Continental philosophy is also a part of contemporary philosophy, and this changes how we understand philosophical reasoning by exploring why we think the way we do. Logic and reason are often important in continental philosophy, focusing on the specific language philosophers use to express their ideas, but with a modern twist. Modern philosophers often use real-life examples and practical ethics to discuss past issues. These issues don't automatically get solved just by looking at them in a modern way.

There are two exceptions to the idea that modern problems are problems from the past and that our understanding of them has just changed: environmental ethics/rights and artificial intelligence. Environmental ethics, also called conservation, is a new concept if we look at the history of philosophy itself. Artificial intelligence is naturally a new type of philosophy because computers and programming only became popular in the mid-1980s. Previous philosophers didn't need to worry about a computer with ethics as there weren't computers or phones that did your thinking for you.

Artificial Intelligence

Artificial intelligence has gained popularity since the start of contemporary thinking because people need a new way to understand their world. There are quite a few things to consider when asking questions about contemporary philosophy. Finding answers to these questions will help us move away from the fear of the unknown. Understanding artificial intelligence is done by asking questions about current topics from a physical perspective:

- Considering society: AI programming is influenced by the social rules of the person who created the program. How sure are we that the AI isn't biased (having a belief in something based on personal preferences instead of logic)? (Metaphysics)

- Ethics: How will a program or robot know right from wrong? (Ethics)

- Impact on learning: How will AI help you with homework? If the AI does the work for you, who will know? (Morality)

- Industry and jobs: If a robot can do the work your parents do in half the amount of time and for a quarter of their salary, the robots will take their jobs, which leaves them in a difficult position. (The state of nature)

- Responsibility: Who is responsible for the actions of the AI program or robot, and who will take the blame if something goes wrong? (Rationalism)

- Security: Can AI influence security systems and monitor us without our consent? (Autonomy)

The question of safety and protection is a vital part of jobs for humans. It's different for robots and AI. AI-controlled cars are becoming more popular now. From a philosophical standpoint, the question of which laws they follow starts surfacing in manufacturing areas. How do they control the speed if every country has a different speed limit? If the car runs a red light and injures someone, who is responsible? More importantly, how can we ensure the AI used in cars and other places focuses on the common good of the people? If the AI doesn't understand what the "common good" is, how will it know the difference between the common good and a crime?

If robots don't feel pain, should they still be protected? Robots and AI programs don't exist in a separate space from us, and we have to share our resources with them (even if they don't eat). Power and energy are finite (something that can be used up), and the technology needed for AI and robots uses a lot of power and covers large areas of the land previously occupied by animals and plants.

AI in philosophy has more questions than answers at this stage, but AI and robots are still young compared to other philosophical concepts. In time, these questions will be answered, and your future can be alongside AI and robots, like your ancestors' past was alongside animals and their community.

Equal Representation in Philosophy: Feminism

To understand feminist philosophy, we have to understand what feminism means. There are different types of feminism, including political feminism and philosophical feminism. In politics, feminism means equality—equal rights to vote and equal say in what happens to their lives and families without needing a man to make these decisions for them. Before 1923, women weren't allowed to ask for a divorce, and in some families, women whose husbands had died weren't allowed to re-marry unless their in-laws (spouse's parents) gave her permission.

That might sound odd now, but before the start of contemporary thinking, unmarried women were very limited in what they could do. They weren't allowed to own property (including examples of philosophical property spoken of earlier in the book) and were banned from important places and events unless they had a husband. Events like this included parties held by prominent families in the community or political debates where the men discussed government and community issues. These examples removed their autonomy for themselves and their children, and because they weren't able to contribute equally, the philosophical questions they had were ignored in favor of what people thought they needed (without asking them first).

Philosophical feminism was started by Simone de Beauvoir, and she focused on a combined version of politics and the philosophical method of cause and effect of an idea and an understanding of how we think.

Feminist philosophy is about allowing people to make their own choices about their bodies and health, knowing what is right and wrong when it comes to friends and family instead of just listening to the government or rules, and making sure that women's opinions are heard when discussing important issues.

Women weren't recognized initially because people assumed they didn't have anything to add, but they were recognized as a group after publishing their own works and philosophies independently. Women and the feminist philosophical idea were further recognized when they identified the weakness in traditional philosophy: The exclusion of disabled people and those whose political philosophies went against the government. Feminist philosophy shined a new light on alternative modes of thinking, which started an entirely new era of thought: The era of inclusion.

Humane Contemporary Philosophy: Animal and Environmental Rights

Early philosophers focused on politics and ethics because this influenced how their community operated. Animals and livestock weren't really considered as pets or companions. Only the rich could afford pets because they were the only ones who could feed their animals and afford to build walls to keep the dogs safe. Animals, including dogs, cattle, sheep, pigs, chickens, and in some places in the Middle East, camels were used as farm animals for food and used to pull farming equipment like plows and threshers. Dogs were used as protection from wolves and other predatory animals, but they didn't sleep inside on a cozy bed. They slept outside with the rest of the farm animals.

Another reason animals were used for livestock and protection was that people didn't think animals could feel pain or have a personality of their own. Humans and animals lived completely separately, and it wasn't until the early 1980s that people started viewing animals as pets instead of beasts of burden (another word people used for farm animals). Modern philosophers like Freya Mathews supported the idea of animals with autonomy, and she urged world governments to encourage people to include animals in their daily lives. She argued that this would give people a better understanding of modern ethics when seen through the animal's eyes.

From her arguments and others who agreed with her ideas, animals and humans started gaining equal rights—no killing of animals unless it's for food, no harming an animal, and no using the animals for your benefit if the animal becomes distressed. The animal rights movement started changing how animals were treated in movies, and their habitats were also protected so they could live out their lives free from fear of people harming them or taking over their land. This includes the protection of the environment and the insects and plants in the area. Contemporary philosophy argues that all creatures part of an environment need protection, and governments have to ensure this happens.

Justice Must Prevail: Philosophy and the Law

Philosophy and education go hand-in-hand. When the police and law get involved, this is even more important. The police in your city are responsible for stopping crime when they see it and protecting those who follow the law. They have to answer to the judge and other law-enforcement officials.

Philosophy and the law also have an international component. International law is very close to political philosophy because the laws deal with how people understand their world, the types of questions they ask, what rights they have as citizens of a country, and how people are expected to behave in the state of nature. Unlike states and governments that use the police to keep people as part of their political community, international law doesn't have a single police force. Each state must use its own police force so the decisions made for them follow their personal philosophies and ethical standpoints.

For example, in countries like Germany and the Netherlands, you or your parents wouldn't be allowed to clip your bird's wings or dock your dog's tail (removing a piece of the tail to make it look nicer) because both of these procedures are considered animal cruelty, based on a philosopher's input when the laws of the countries were made. The police and judges in those countries have to follow the regional laws as part of the European Union. If you clip your bird's wings or dock your dog's tail and someone reports you, the police have the authority to arrest your parents, and a judge can make them pay a fine. These laws aren't international laws, though, and in the US, some vets will allow wing clipping and tail docking based on your preference. They still have to follow the general international animal laws based on discussions about death (bioethics) and access to food (doing your duty as the animal's guardian).

Modern-Day Chemistry: Philosophy and Medicine

Questions about philosophy and medicine, called bioethics, can be difficult to answer (and ask) because, unlike the other types of contemporary philosophy and the questions asked earlier in the book, these types of questions are always personal, and they might affect more than one family member at a time. In general, philosophical questions deal with the deep questions about reality, morality, religion, spirituality, and how we understand the past, but bioethical questions deal with death, autonomy as people age, and the questions people in doctor's clinics are too afraid to ask. They might not know how to ask for the answers they need, or they might not know who to trust.

Bioethical issues relate to problems and laws regarding the medical community (doctors, nurses, hospital staff) and you or your family as the patients. Bioethics is a part of every law and process in all countries, but not all countries share the same rights and privileges as their neighbor. For example, in the US, male circumcision is legal in all states. It's still up to the doctor: If the doctor doesn't feel comfortable performing the male circumcision, the parents of the child can't do anything to persuade them, and if they do, they could get into a lot of trouble. In Iceland, it is completely illegal, and a doctor who performs a circumcision on a boy will lose their license to practice medicine and will most likely go to jail.

Think about it: When people we love get old, they often lose the ability to do the things they were so good at when they were young. If your grandparent loved driving you to the park or library, they will still be that person when they are old, and they will still enjoy doing those things with you. The only difference is that they might not be able to see the road as clearly, or their reaction time (very important for driving) might not be what it once was. As a family, your parents, aunts, and uncles might have to ask your grandparent to stop driving because it isn't safe anymore. Getting old and losing the ability to do what they used to do isn't anyone's fault. It happens, and the only thing you and your family can do is help your grandparent keep as much autonomy (freedom) as they can. As we have seen in this book, autonomy is linked to personality. From a contemporary perspective, medicine and philosophy are important because of how modern laws and freedoms affect the medical community and the citizens who contribute to the political community.

Keep Thinking! Suggested Questions

Remember, there are no wrong answers to philosophical questions!

- What do you think "a current issue" means?

- What does analysis mean?

- What is modern philosophy?

- What is conservation?

- What is a philosophical work?

- What is the difference between ethics, political philosophy, and moral philosophy?

- What is an endangered species?

- What is animal welfare?

- What is a medical issue?

- What is feminism?

Chapter 10:

Questions and Activities

Philosophy is Fun!

The fun part about philosophy is you can test almost all the theories out using simple questions and activities like those that the first thinkers used to gain people's trust. Isn't that cool? By asking the right questions and acting out the answers as activities, we can better understand why these questions are so important in the first place. There are lots of important questions in this book; let's look at them more closely.

Write these questions and answers in the philosophy book you started at the beginning of this book. Any activity can be used for any of the questions below. Don't worry about repeating activities for a chapter! All activities count because all forms of knowledge are valid. There are general guidelines for the activities, so you can mix and match whatever or whoever you like! The way you create these activities will benefit you long after you leave school because you can use different methods to come to a conclusion, just like the philosophers in this book did many, many years ago.

Get Your Thinking Cap On With Chapter Questions!

Each chapter has a questionnaire section that follows the general theme of the chapter. Questions from Chapter One are called The First Question because the first important questions from the Greek and

Roman periods were answered. Questions from Chapter Two are called The Second Age because this chapter introduced you to the second age of philosophical questioning by the church. Chapter Three deals with Islam, so the questions for that chapter are under The Third Star, and so on.

The First Question:

Do you know of any important buildings in Ancient Greece?

If you were a Greek deity, which field of philosophy would you choose to govern over and why?

Do you want to travel one day?

If so, would you focus on places with historical significance or areas that look nice?

Should the law be applied to those who make the law?

Do you think how a country is run should be separate from how people understand the world?

Is time important?

Why or why not?

The Second Age:

Why is it called the Middle East?

How far is the Middle East from Greece?

Will this distance make a difference to philosophy?

Should kings, queens, and presidents control the church?

The Third Star:

Are India and the Middle East on the same continent?

Are the libraries you see today the same as the libraries from the ancient world?

How do people gain influence over others?

Do you think science and kindness are different from one another?

The Fourth Good Question:

Do you think all humans are part of a community?

Why is protection important?

Do you think you have an identity?

If yes, how do you know? If not, why do you think that is?

Do you think autonomy is important?

The Fifth Reality:

How can you be sure that something exists?

Do you think memories are real?

Why or why not?

Can we experience reality through our experiences alone?

Do you think your dreams mean anything?

Why or why not?

Do you think doubting something will make it easier to believe afterward?

Where do you think your thoughts come from?

The Sixth Deed:

Do you think helping someone is part of your morality?

Do you have a will? (Not a legal will.)

Do you think deception is always bad?

Do you think ethics are important in a community?

Why or why not?

Why is property (including philosophical property) important to people?

Why are rights important?

Do you think freedom is always an option?

The Seventh Healing Question:

Why is it important to focus on the practical nature of a philosophy?

Does everything have to have a beginning?

Why or why not?

Are titles (Lord, Lady, Master, Mistress, etc.) important?

Does education mean understanding?

Please explain.

Do you think spirits and gods are the same thing?

Why or why not?

Do you think everything and everyone needs protection?

Why or why not?

Do you think ancestors are important?

Why or why not?

Is it normal to be scared for the future?

Why do you think the elderly should be protected?

Why do you think people have negative thoughts?

The Eighth Way of Life:

Do you think seeing something helps with understanding?

Do you think enlightenment is possible?

Why or why not?

Should food be prepared by the person eating it?

Do we have multiple lifetimes?

Should religion be a personal quest?

Why or why not?

In your religion or culture, why do impurities exist?

Why do you think the kami exist in our world?

How many religions are there in India?

Why did the Buddha teach acceptance?

Why is intoxication a bad thing?

The Ninth Contemporary:

Do you think continental philosophy and the way philosophy is practiced and taught on your continent mean the same thing?

How do you think our minds work?

Why do you think people didn't recognize animals as important in the early days?

Do you think animals and humans should have the same rights?

Do you think a doctor can do something illegal even though they are a doctor?

Why or why not?

Why do you think bioethical issues are difficult to discuss?

Do you think people will want to be treated the same way throughout their lives?

Why or why not?

Do you think feminism is always necessary?

Why or why not?

Do you think women should be in control of their bodies at all times?

Why or why not?

Do you think disabled people should be allowed to participate in the political community?

Why or why not?

Do you think a robot has a concept of self?

Why or why not?

Do you think robots should be protected?

Do you think it's fair that robots take dangerous jobs away from humans?

Why or why not?

Options for the Activities:

Option One

Look at Google Maps or a map book (the bigger the map book, the better) and find the important areas for the chapters in question.

- How are the countries connected?

- Can you see the old country lines (of the ancient world) compared to now?

Ask your parents for a long sheet of paper and complete a timeline of the philosophers discussed in the chapter. If you do this with multiple chapters, compare the timelines between philosophers and eras.

Ask your parents or teacher to help you make a word-search activity for each chapter. All information is important, so don't worry about adding seemingly unimportant words! Five words per heading should do the trick.

Option Two

Make a visual mind map for each chapter or a chapter of your choice, and write important dates and philosophies on the connecting lines. You can do this with pen and paper or mind-map tools on the internet.

Option Three

For the chapters that deal with deities, kami, God, or Allah, make a list of what seems important for those beings. Then, on another sheet of paper, make a list of what you would do or promote if you were all-powerful.

- Are the two lists similar?

- Why or why not?

Option Four

Ask your parents or teacher to find pictures of your favorite philosophers from the book, and ask them to print out small pictures (about 1.5-inch squares).

Place these pictures next to items in your home that you think the philosophers would find important if they lived with you.

Ask yourself:

1. Why would this item be important for this philosopher?

2. Why is it important to me?

Option Five

Use a ruler or your finger to cover random words from any two or three questions from a chapter or the whole book, and start a new question with the words you can still see. I'll give an example:

Questions from chapters:

1. Do you know of any important buildings in ancient Greece?

2. Do you think how a country is run should be separate from how people understand the world?

3. Should the law apply the same to everyone, including the people who make the law?

If you blocked off the words **buildings**, **separate**, and **include**, your new questions could be:

1. Was Greece important? *or* Why was Greece Important?

2. Should how a country is run be explained to everyone else so their laws can be understood by the rest of the world?

3. Should making the laws affect everyone?

Questions from chapters:

1. Do you think science and kindness are very different from one another?

2. Do you think kings, queens, and presidents should be in control of the church?

3. Do you have an identity?

If you blocked off the words **science**, **presidents**, and **have**, your new questions could be:

1. What makes kindness different from everything else?

2. Should the church control kings and queens?

3. What is an identity?

By swapping and changing the questions using this method, it will be a very long time before you run out of questions. All philosophical questions can be asked and answered in a variety of ways based on what you are looking for and who you are asking. There might be no wrong answers in philosophy, but that also means there are no wrong questions!

As you answer all of these questions (even if you don't make activities out of them), think about how the people of the time would have answered. This will help you understand their way of thinking!

Conclusion

Everything has a beginning, but not everything has an end. This is even more true for philosophy and wisdom: The questions and opportunities for learning never end. From the first word spoken by our ancestors to the first word recorded to track livestock, people have asked questions about the beginning of something. People also ask these questions with a goal in mind—to find the end of their questions for the day!

Imagine this: A small cave in Greece in a clearing with only one entrance. This cave is a cave of wonders, even more so than the Cave of Wonders in *Aladdin*. This cave might not have mountains of gold and jewels or a mischievous rug with a lamp, but it has something better! It has the answer to a question people didn't know how to ask: What happens when we get stuck in a cave our entire lives, never seeing the sun or the trees that give us life? The cave in this story is Plato's cave, and to understand what happens in the cave, we have to think of the cave as a real cave filled with people, lights, and knowledge. (Yes, this is a very big cave!)

By imagining ancient philosophical issues as direct or physical problems like the cave, it will be easier to come to a solution. When you imagine something in your head (or draw it if you struggle to visualize things), the issues and questions from the philosophers in this book would be focused on how they were asked in their own time—Plato was the only one who thought like that at the time. In his cave, he was alone. You can visualize the solution easily. The cave in Plato's story marked the beginning of questions being asked in Greece and, as you saw in the book, the beginning of questions asked in the Western world.

Let's move across to Italy and Baghdad, where the first religious philosophers started out, a far cry from the early days of Greek philosophers. Religious philosophy is used to help people understand the world from the eyes of their God or Allah, and it's also used to make compelling arguments from different philosophical perspectives. Questions have existed for a lot longer than people could write them down, and ancient societies (anything older than 2500-3000 years ago) had familiar troubles and questions to what modern people have. These troubles and questions include:

- The troubles related to predators in the wilderness before fences and traps.

- The trouble of morality and the right way to live.

- The troubles of autonomy and rights related to your actions and possessions.

- The troubles relating to the question of how ancient people knew who they could trust to lead them

- The troubles regarding the question of who made the decisions for their lives when it influenced the community in general?

- The troubles of how and why their children were educated?

These troubles and questions all had a beginning, but how people answered them and how they are answered today relates to what people choose to believe.

Nature is cool! In philosophy, there is also the nature of people and how we behave when our troubles don't seem to go away, like the annoying "Beep! Beep! Beep!" on our alarm clocks in the morning. If only there was a solution to sleepy mornings! By addressing our human nature as part of our community, we can help those around us by understanding what's expected of us and what's expected of others.

Speaking of dreaming, have you wondered what reality is? How do you know what you know? Like the lines of your books or games on the shelf. Everything you read and absorb can change how you see your reality. In philosophy, every reality is valid for those who experience it. Your reality might be different compared to your friend down the road because you have different life experiences. Your life experiences change your reality!

Responsibility. Really? Why do I need to be responsible? I'm only a child! Well, from now on, you can call yourself a philosopher because you were responsible enough to finish this book! Immanuel Kant would have been proud. You did your duty as a philosopher to ask questions and search for the answers within your reach. Not all philosophical topics can be as easily discussed as they were in this book. This isn't anyone's fault. Philosophy has been around for nearly 3000 years; it's impossible to be responsible for every question and answer ever asked.

Far to the East, there were sages who taught about balance, family, and education. These thinkers spread Chinese culture and philosophies to the ends of the earth. Their philosophies were picked up by Western universities like Oxford, Cambridge, and the University of Paris as a way to understand the mysticism around culture and worldview that was completely different from their own. Confucius and Lao Tzu taught their modest yet progressive philosophies approximately 1500 years before the West acknowledged the importance of other types of thinking.

As for the spirits, who knew you could have a spirit in your home looking after your plants and ensuring your water is safe to drink? Don't forget to thank them by offering sweets! As we walk down the path of wisdom and philosophy, meditation and contemplation could help us understand all the connecting theories and changing times. Asking questions about what we see on the side of the road and what we experience in our daily lives helps us think about our lives without focusing on our reflections in the mirror. If we focus on the reflections of others, we could spend more time on things that matter.

This leads us to the final part of the book: The important questions of today. These can be answered from a few different perspectives:

- The perspective of others.

- The perspective of an animal.

- A robot's perspective (how cool!).

- The understanding of someone who experiences life one day at a time.

- The understanding of a judge whose job is to balance the scales of philosophy and the law.

Asking questions is what philosophers do, and the answers to these questions can come from anywhere. A book, a person, an animal, or a political theory that runs your government. By asking questions, you understand the world around you a little differently and a little better. Go forth and ponder!

References

Adamson, P. (2018). *Al-Kindi* . Stanford Encyclopedia of Philosophy. https://plato.stanford.edu/entries/al-kindi/

Ahmed, B., F. Pasnau., R. Pasnau (2021, June 23). *Ibn Rushd [Averroes]*. Stanford   Encyclopedia   of   Philosophy. https://plato.stanford.edu/entries/ibn-rushd/

Baxter, F. (2022, July 22). *What is modern and contemporary philosophy?* Pondering   Philosopher. https://www.ponderingphilosopher.com/what-is-modern-and-contemporary-philosophy-2/

Beauchamp, T. L., Walters, L., Khan, J. P., & Mastroianni, A. C. (2014). *Contemporary issues in bioethics* (Eighth, pp. 24–29). Wadsworth Cengage Learning.

Bertram, C. (2010, September 27). *Jean Jacques Rousseau*. Stanford Encyclopedia   of   Philosophy. https://plato.stanford.edu/entries/rousseau/

Brennan, A., & Lo, Y.-S. (2021, December 3). *Environmental ethics*. Stanford   Encyclopedia   of   Philosophy. https://plato.stanford.edu/entries/ethics-environmental/

Brickhouse, T., & Smith, N. D. (2015). *Plato*. Internet Encyclopedia of Philosophy. https://iep.utm.edu/plato/

Brink, D. (2007, October 9). *Mill's moral and political philosophy*. Stanford Encyclopedia   of   Philosophy. https://plato.stanford.edu/entries/mill-moral-political/

Brooks, T. (2021, June 3). *Hegel's social and political philosophy*. Stanford Encyclopedia   of   Philosophy. https://plato.stanford.edu/entries/hegel-social-political/#Mora

Brown, W. T. (2002, December). *Introduction to Buddhism*. Stanford Encyclopedia of Philosophy. https://spice.fsi.stanford.edu/docs/introduction_to_buddhism

Cheng, A. (2005). The problem with "Chinese philosophy." *Revue Internationale de Philosophie*, *232*(2), 175–180. https://doi.org/10.3917/rip.232.0175

Chenu, M.-D. (2019, April 28). *St. Thomas Aquinas*. Encyclopædia Britannica. https://www.britannica.com/biography/Saint-Thomas-Aquinas

Clayton, E. (n.d.). *Cicero*. Internet Encyclopedia of Philosophy. https://iep.utm.edu/cicero-roman-philosopher/

Csikszentmihalyi, M. (2020, March 31). *Confucius*. Stanford Encyclopedia of Philosophy. https://plato.stanford.edu/entries/confucius/

Curd, P. (2016, March 10). *Presocratic philosophy*. Encyclopædia Britannica. https://plato.stanford.edu/entries/presocratics/

Doug. (2009, February 25). *Introduction to Shinto religion*. Japan Life and Religion. http://japanlifeandreligion.com/2009/02/25/introduction-to-shinto-religion/

DRBU Staff. (2023, November 16). *Intro to Buddhism: What are the five Buddhist precepts?* Dharma Realm Buddhist University. https://www.drbu.edu/news/intro-to-buddhism-what-are-the-five-buddhist-precepts/

Gutas, D. (2016, September 15). *Ibn Sina [Avicenna]*. Stanford Encyclopedia of Philosophy. https://plato.stanford.edu/entries/ibn-sina/

Hardwick, N. A. (2011, March 1). *Rousseau and the social contract tradition*. E-International Relations. https://www.e-ir.info/2011/03/01/rousseau-and-the-social-contract-tradition/

Harrison, V. S. (2008, September). *Eastern philosophy*. Reading Religion. https://readingreligion.org/9781138215788/eastern-philosophy/

Ho, D. Y. F. (1995). Selfhood and identity in Confucianism, Taoism, Buddhism, and Hinduism: Contrasts with the west. *Journal for the Theory of Social Behaviour*, *25*(2), 115–139. https://www.humiliationstudies.org/documents/HoSelfhooda ndIdentityinConfucianismTaoismBuddhismandHinduism.pdf

Hussain, W. (2018, February 26). *The common good*. Stanford Encyclopedia of Philosophy. https://plato.stanford.edu/entries/common-good/

Johnson, R., & Cureton, A. (2004, February 23). *Kant's moral philosophy*. Stanford Encyclopedia of Philosophy. https://plato.stanford.edu/entries/kant-moral/

Kamtekar, R. (2018). *Marcus Aurelius* (E. N. Zalta, Ed.). Stanford Encyclopedia of Philosophy. https://plato.stanford.edu/entries/marcus-aurelius/

Lake, T. (2021, October 26). *Socrates' philosophy: The ancient Greek philosopher and his legacy*. The Collector. https://www.thecollector.com/socrates-philosophy-ancient-greek-philosopher-legacy/

Mark, J. (2020, July 9). *Lao-Tzu*. World History Encyclopedia. https://www.worldhistory.org/Lao-Tzu/

Markie, P. (2004, August 19). *Rationalism vs. Empiricism* . Stanford Encyclopedia of Philosophy. https://plato.stanford.edu/entries/rationalism-empiricism/#IntuThes

Matsuyama, H. (2022, November 29). *Shintoism essential value: Impurity and purification rituals*. Patternz. https://www.patternz.jp/shintoism-essential-value-impurity-and-purification-rituals/

McAfee, N. (2018, June 28). *Feminist philosophy*. Stanford Encyclopedia of Philosophy. https://plato.stanford.edu/entries/feminist-philosophy/

McGinnis, J., & Acar, R. (2023, May 31). *Arabic and Islamic philosophy of religion*. Stanford Encyclopedia of Philosophy. https://plato.stanford.edu/entries/arabic-islamic-religion/

Müller, V. C. (2020, April 30). *Ethics of artificial intelligence and robotics*. Stanford Encyclopedia of Philosophy. https://plato.stanford.edu/entries/ethics-ai/

Nel, H. (2020, October 13). *Research methods for Ph. D. and master's degree studies: Rationalism*. Intgrty. https://www.intgrty.co.za/tag/innate-concept-thesis/

O'Donnell, J. (2019, May 23). *Saint Augustine*. Encyclopædia Britannica. https://www.britannica.com/biography/Saint-Augustine

Oppy, G. (2020). *Ontological arguments* (E. N. Zalta, Ed.). Stanford Encyclopedia of Philosophy. https://plato.stanford.edu/entries/ontological-arguments/#:~:text=Anselm%20claims%20to%20derive%20the

Pries, L., Lawrence, F., Delaney, R., Smith, D., Furst, C., & Bynum, R. (n.d.). *Philosophy of punishment, justice, and cultural conflict in criminal justice*. Police Chief Magazine. https://www.policechiefmagazine.org/philosophy-punishment-justice-cultural-conflict-criminal-justice/

Rahman, F., & Schimmel, A. (n.d.). *Islam - Critiques, theology, Aristotle*. Encyclopædia Britannica. https://www.britannica.com/topic/Islam/Critiques-of-Aristotle-in-Islamic-theology

Roughley, N. (2021, March 15). *Human nature*. Stanford Encyclopedia of Philosophy. https://plato.stanford.edu/entries/human-nature/

Sockolov, M. (2017, December 9). *Understanding the different types of Buddhism*. One Mind Dharma. https://oneminddharma.com/types-of-buddhism/

Solmsen, F. (2024, June 4). *Hesiod. Encyclopedia Britannica*. https://www.britannica.com/biography/Hesiod

Stumpf, S. E., & Abel, D. C. (2001). *Elements of philosophy* (Fourth). McGraw-Hill.

Taoism. (2014). Bbc.co.uk. https://www.bbc.co.uk/religion/religions/taoism/

The Wise Apple. (2024, March 6). *Confucianism*. National Geographic. https://education.nationalgeographic.org/resource/confucianism/

Thomas Aquinas. (n.d.). Home.csulb.edu. https://home.csulb.edu/~cwallis/100/aquinas.html

Truncellito, D. (n.d.). *Epistemology*. Internet Encyclopedia of Philosophy. https://iep.utm.edu/epistemo/

Tuckness, A. (2005, November 9). *Locke's political philosophy*. Stanford Encyclopedia of Philosophy. https://plato.stanford.edu/entries/locke-political/

Vogt, K. (2015). *Seneca*. Stanford Encyclopedia of Philosophy. https://plato.stanford.edu/entries/seneca/

Williams, T. (2015). *Saint Anselm*. Stanford Encyclopedia of Philosophy. https://plato.stanford.edu/entries/anselm/

www.ingramcontent.com/pod-product-compliance
Lightning Source LLC
Chambersburg PA
CBHW071452070426
42452CB00039B/1173